A Young Preacher Goes to Seminary

D1641545

Dr. Charles A. Crane
2021

A Young Preacher Goes to Seminary
is available at special quantity discounts for bulk purchase
for sales promotions, premiums, fund-raising, and educational
needs.

For details write
Endurance Press, 577 N Cardigan Ave, Star ID 83669.
Visit Endurance Press' website at *www.endurancepress.com*

A Young Preacher Goes to Seminary

PUBLISHED BY ENDURANCE PRESS
577 N Cardigan Ave
Star, ID 83669 U.S.A.

All views expressed within are the view of the author and
do not necessarily reflect the views of the publisher.

L.C.
Printed in the U.S.A.

Contents

Preface

The purpose of the young preacher series of books is to illustrate just how important the preaching ministry really is to humanity, our nation, and our modern culture. Too often preachers have been portrayed as sort of a sub-standard group of humans. Do they actually wear clergy clothes or neckties to bed at night? Do they have a judgmental comment to make about anything that is fun? Do they contribute anything worthwhile to our culture that makes life better?

Having given my life to the preaching ministry and also having helped train the next generation of preachers, I believe my inside view may help to remove the negative view of the preaching profession. Yes, like any profession, not all preachers are worthy of respect, but the majority are.

What is the work of the preacher? They are educators; teaching things that are the foundation for civilization, like honesty, kindness, love, morality, generosity, care for the sick, poor, and about eternal life. They offer one of the finest educational schools in most towns, without people being taxed to pay for it. They are called Sunday schools, or youth meetings. Preachers marry people, bury the dead, counsel those hurting or in trouble, up-hold the sanctity of marriage, law and order. The church has been the first to provide for medical needs around the world, by providing nursing and hospitals. Many of our finest hospitals and colleges were begun by preachers and churches. The list of all the good provided by the church and ministry is too long to list here.

The stories that are told in this book are all true to the best of my memory. Since the events are from so long ago, it is probable that some of the names and exact sequences may be somewhat foggy in my mind. Some names have been changed to protect people's privacy. Some names have been preserved since the people deserve to be remembered for their perversity. The events all really happened. The people are real. Over-all, the communities were blessed because a young preacher was doing his best to point people to Jesus and eternal life.

My prayer is that these stories will not only entertain you, but make clear how supremely important the preaching ministry really is. In fact America will be in serious danger if there is not another wave of great preachers that lead us to a nationwide revival.

The Young Preacher Goes to Seminary

Why Leave Salt Lake City?

After seven-and-one-half years of ministry in Salt Lake City, both Margaret and I were almost totally burned out. Most of the time, we worked for more than 60 hours each week. We prayed, taught, led, faced the constant efforts of the LDS to win our members, spoke, counseled, and were both almost totally exhausted.

Everywhere I went I was asked to talk about the Mormon religion, give workshops about Mormonism, asked to talk with the missionaries and to tutor preachers and church leaders about LDS issues. My heart was in preaching the gospel of Jesus Christ and His church, not just fighting this vigorous cult. Sometimes I felt like I was trying to stop the incoming ocean tide.

Dr. Wayne Shaw saw my dilemma and encouraged me to take a break. At that time Ernie Chamberlain asked me to lead a revival meeting at First Christian Church in Caldwell, Idaho. I was to preach and Ray Renzema was to lead the singing and sing solos. The meeting was blessed by God with good attendance and many came to accept Christ. It was hard work but also refreshing, since I was doing what I loved most, preaching Jesus Christ as Savior and Lord.

On the last day of the meeting, Brother Chamberlain asked me into his church office. He said his purpose was to encourage me to go to Seminary. I confessed that I was about burned out in Utah. As we concluded our meeting he got me to promise that I would go to Seminary. He said it would prepare me for the greater role he believed that God had for my life. I gave him my promise to do so.

A few months later Margaret and I made the decision to resign and pursue higher education, either at Lincoln Christian Seminary, or Emmanuel School of Religion. Leaving Utah was a tough decision, but after much talk and prayer we made a firm decision to do so.

Seeking New Employment

My Bible College training had extended to six-and-one-half years, due to poor planning on my part in taking the required classes. This was why my Bachelor of Sacred Literature degree resulted in 158 hours of earned credit, instead of the required 128 hours.

The Bachelor of Sacred Literature degree there also required a Thesis which should amount to at least an additional 12 hours of credit. This was high quality education, but left me still feeling only marginally qualified for my life's work of ministry. Are not people's spiritual needs as important as their physical ones?

These extra hours of undergraduate education often helped in the work of ministry, but they also induced a desire to continue going to school for advanced degrees. Often people would ask me questions I could not answer, questions like "Where did Cain get his wife?" or "What is the mark of Cain?" or some such thing.

This had been one of our motives in leaving Oregon and going to Salt Lake City, Utah. But we learned, after arriving in Salt Lake City, that Utah had no quality advanced training for theological degrees.

The best available to me in Utah was on-line study from Johnson Christian University in Tennessee and I did enroll in some classes there. Then the next year Emmanuel Christian Seminary offered some extension classes in Portland, Oregon, that I took. These classes also fueled my desire for further study and underlined the value of further learning.

My goal for additional schooling was the desire to provide congregants with capable and quality leadership. One area where I felt a need was having better material for preaching. Each Sunday I was constantly scraping the bottom of the barrel for something to preach.

With the encouragement of Dr. Wayne Shaw, Dr. Max Ward Randall, and Ernie Chamberlain, I finally decided to make the move to Seminary. Even when leaving Utah, I had not fully decided on which Seminary to attend. Lincoln Christian Seminary and Emmanuel School of Religion were both urging me to attend there. Both had high quality programs.

To attend Seminary meant that I needed to have a ministry close enough to the Seminary so I could drive to and from school each week and also support my family.

Both schools sent me prospective churches that were looking for preachers. There were five churches that wanted to interview me. Three were near Lincoln and two were near Emmanuel.

I chose the one that seemed best suited for our needs and we for theirs and also that was closest to the Seminary. We traveled there to be interviewed.

You've Been Hired

I ended up being interviewed by the eldership at Moweaqua Christian Church in central Illinois. This interview still remains clear in my mind. I was asked all sorts of questions, both personal and doctrinal. After about one-and-one-half hours the chairman called for a vote; resulting in a unanimous call for me to be their new preacher. They said, "You are hired, go to the church office right now and call the other churches and tell them you are now employed."

I replied, "Isn't it necessary for the congregation to also vote on this?" They replied, "Yes it is, but if they do not accept you we will all resign as elders. We know our church and they will love you."

When the congregation voted, there was only one no vote out of the hundreds cast. Two different people later told me they voted no, since they knew it would be very positive and they didn't want me to have a big head. I learned later that neither had voted no. I never learned who the one person who did was, but maybe it was Evelyn. Evelyn???

You Work Too Hard

When it was time to move to Illinois it was another of those sad times of separation from all the dearly loved Christians in Salt Lake City. Our time in Salt Lake City had been mostly wonderful in the church. Nearing the end of our ministry, the Elders had given me a $600 a month raise in salary and said I had to show receipts for half of this raise being spent on recreation since all I did was work.

We decided to buy a small travel trailer that we could pull behind our 1971 Chevrolet Malibu that had a big engine. We began to use it and enjoyed it very much. It had beds for all five of us, bathroom, toilet, range, refrigerator, and everything so we could camp with comfort. We frequently used it for two- or three-day camping trips.

When it was time to leave for Illinois, this trailer was a blessing since we had a place to eat and sleep as we traveled across America to our new home. On the way we stopped at a city park that was in the center of a small town in Kansas to fix and eat lunch in the park.

Our holding tanks were full of grey and black water (sewage is called black). We had parked our trailer right near a storm drain at the side of the street. So I asked one of the boys to drain the grey water, but instead he drained both tanks. I looked and here was all this filth draining into the gutter and running slowly to the storm drain. At that moment the local sheriff drove by looking us over. I hastily closed the drains and we left rapidly. The evidence of our visit remained in the gutter.

Margaret was driving the car and pulling the trailer, a friend was driving Margaret's car and I was driving the U-Haul truck. While we were traveling, a storm came up with such high winds that the trailer was about to blow over. The wind was so strong even small gravel was blowing through the air. We had to pull off of the road and face it into the wind to keep it from being blown over.

Margaret had bravely agreed to try to drive the car and trailer to Illinois, but she was not prepared for such extreme conditions. She was in tears with trying to pull the trailer. But with God's blessing we finally arrived in Moweaqua.

Moweaqua, Illinois

They told me that the word Moweaqua was an Indian word that meant muddy water. That seemed appropriate since a creek that was called "Flat Branch" sort of ran through town to the south. It was wide and shallow and often muddy, especially on the shore lines. It did not remind me of the rushing and clear streams out West in Utah, Idaho, and Oregon.

The town was distinguished by tall grain elevators that were on each side of the railroad tracks that ran through town north and south. These elevators were huge to hold the abundant crops that were harvested each fall as the area is one of the most productive farming areas anywhere in America.

The top soil is 10–20 feet deep and the frequent summer rain storms made things grow so fast in the summer that one can hear corn growing on a humid summer evening. Stand quiet and listen and one can hear it sort of snap and pop.

The humid summer heat was also conducive to excellent conditions for growing crops or gardens. I tried to grow fruit and tomatoes in Utah with only modest success. Having been raised on a farm in Oregon I decided to work up one of the flower beds in the back yard of the parsonage to raise some tomatoes.

This bed was about 4 X 6 feet. I planted six tomato plants there and the first farmer that came by laughed right out loud at me. I asked what was wrong and he said with a chuckle, "You will see." When the plants grew they were a jungle and in the fall before the first freeze I picked 120 ripe tomatoes off the six plants.

The humid weather made summer time rather uncomfortable. One day while playing softball on the church team, perspiration was running off of the tail of my shirt in a trickle. We had to air out our bedding each morning then it would dry out so we could sleep in it again that night and it would not mildew.

The streets of the village were lined with huge trees and the lawns were verdant and always green. There was no need of sprinkler systems or watering things with a hose. People took pride in their homes and they were beautifully maintained and well painted.

The business district consisted of the huge grain elevators along the railroad tracks and a row of businesses along each side of the main street. On the west side was a Ford dealership and garage. Next to that to the south was a farm implement dealer. Across the street was the M&W food store. It sat next to the highway and behind it was the church parsonage and Moweaqua Christian Church.

Just north along the highway was Ayers State Bank. Mr. Ayers owned the bank and would freely tell anyone about the net worth of those who banked with him. I tried to deposit the cash I had saved for Seminary with him and so the word went around town that the new preacher was rich.

On the east of the church and parsonage was Macon Street that ran parallel to Highway 51 east one block.

If a person drove north on Macon Street about half a mile they would come to the public schools. Both the grade school and high school were beside each other and covered several acres of ground since they also served people from the surrounding countryside.

Wendall's Restaurant was on the west side of Highway 51 at the north end of town and was the best cared for and prettiest building on the main street. Also on the highway was a bowling alley where a person could buy a soda or snacks. The village was dry and it was against the law to sell alcoholic beverages in town.

The village had a police department with a sheriff, a mortuary, a shoe store and a small hardware store. About the only other thing of significance was the water tower that stood northeast of town surrounded by a gravel parking lot. The town's water came from a well and smelled like propane or oil as Moweaqua was in the middle of an oil field. Some of the members were rich from oil wells on their farms.

Towards the north end of town was a paved road that ran west and east. To the east it came to a town called Shelbyville that sat next to Lake Shelbyville. The lake was created by a dam in the small river that ran through town.

If one drove far enough west they would come to Springfield, the State Capital. Beyond the Mississippi River is Iowa. Southern Illinois has some of the most fertile farm land in the world.

In spite of the humidity, summer storms with lightning and tornadoes, it was one of the most charming places we have ever lived. The blessing to our children was enormous. We thank God for his people in Moweaqua who were such a blessing to our lives.

The last January that we were in Salt Lake City there was seventy-six inches of snow. Many mornings we were faced with a foot or two of snow that had to be shoveled from our driveway before driving.

During the interview with the elders I asked about snow in Illinois. Bernard Carr had responded that most winters one could sweep the snow off the sidewalk and driveway with a broom.

The parsonage garage was down a driveway beside and behind the house. It must have been 250 feet from the street. Imagine my concern when the first snow storm deposited snow drifts five feet deep down the driveway. It took a farmer's tractor with large scoop to clear it so we could get our car out of the garage.

One day when returning from seminary at Lincoln there were huge drifts across the highway. Being used to driving in snow I hit these drifts going fast and somehow managed to get through and back home. They told me it was impossible to make this drive since the highway was closed. Young yes, smart no! But we were used to snow in Utah, where we often drove in it. A foot or two of snow was no excuse for being late somewhere.

The Parsonage

We were to live in the church parsonage which was more than 100 years old. At one time, years before, in its day, it had been a classic beauty of a house, but no longer. We have often commented that the reason the preacher's house is called a "Parsonage" is because it is the place and reason why the parson and wife are prematurely aged ("parson-aged").

Such was the case with our new home. It was a large two-story house that had served as the preacher's house for over one hundred years. It had deferred maintenance evidenced everywhere. A more blunt way of saying this would be to say it was terribly run down.

The roof leaked and large icicles would form out of the walls in the cold winter time. Rain or melting snow water would run down from the leaking roof into the walls, build up ice and the ice would melt on warmer days and water would run out through the siding and form huge icicles down the outside walls and to the ground.

There was a large chimney in the center of the house that had a strong foundation. The house floors were fastened to the solid chimney and the house had settled down so every floor sloped outward from the chimney, both upstairs and down. Drop something round on the floor and it would roll to the outside wall in every room.

Our dining room table was just under the bathroom, which was upstairs. When using the toilet, it would rock back and forth and appear about to fall through the floor and ceiling onto the dining room table below. We joked that if we had an obese guest, their falling through the ceiling was a distinct possibility and possibly right during Sunday dinner. Fortunately, that never happened.

We soon discovered that a hot bath was not possible as the water heater was filled with sediment from the town's bad well water and the heater was three quarters full of lime deposits. I decided to replace the water heater so we could have warm baths. It was so heavy it took several men to help me haul it up out of the basement. It was almost totally full of lime and was heavy as a large rock. Only about three gallons of water drained out of it when I disconnected the water from it, explaining why there was no hot water for baths or for dishes.

The air-conditioning consisted of one downstairs window unit that made little difference in the interior temperature during the hot humid summers, especially in the upstairs bedrooms.

This was during the time of energy shortage and the U.S. President had decreed that thermostats were to be set at no more than 60 degrees in the winter. We wished he would come show us how to get it that warm in the parsonage during the cold winters.

In some ways this old house was charming. It had a porch across the whole front of the house. We were sitting there one evening enjoying a thunder storm when lightning struck a light pole right in front of the house. It scared us silly. The staircase that wound up from the living room and entry was splendid. At one time this house had been fine.

Another plumbing problem manifested itself very soon. The kitchen sink would not drain. It took many minutes for the water to drain out. I knew the probable best solution was for me to repair it. Experience had taught me that parsonage repairs were some of the last things to get attention from the deacons. I got out my tools and crawled back under the house, way back to where the sink drain came through the floor.

I put my pipe wrench on it and gave it a gentle twist and it broke off and the whole pipe fell, from just under the kitchen sink to the cement wall 25 feet away. It broke into three rusty pieces. The last one broke off flush with the outside cement foundation wall where it exited the basement.

What a mess, but with prayer and determination and lots of work it was finally repaired three hours later. I had to chisel a hole through the foundation to remove the old pipe and run the new pipe outside to the drain. I later patched the hole in the foundation. After repair the sink drained, and with the new water heater we now had hot baths. Margaret even had hot water to wash the dishes and the clothes.

Enough Bad News

A Wonderful Christian Community

We left the mission field in Utah and landed in the midst of the Bible Belt. Our new church, according to church records, had over 800 members in a town of about 1,500 people. The sign coming up Highway 51 from the south said population was 1,400 and the one on Highway 51 from the north said 1,500. We never learned the actual fact of the matter.

The church was filled with beautiful and mature Christians. We left behind being constantly beset by the LDS church, to being surrounded by loving Christian people on every side. The church was totally supportive and loving to us except for one lady, "Evelyn," who has earned places in chapters a bit later on if I do not forget.

Pearl Kranz lived next door. Her house was a small bungalow and she came to welcome us with a plate of cookies. She said she loved children and would be happy to tend our three kids whenever needed. She was a retired nurse and in good health. When she learned that both Margaret and I were going to be in school full time she offered to tend our children, since she lived next door. She turned out to be like another grandmother and we and our children loved her.

The main church building was nearly new and was attached to the old church building by a hallway. The old chapel had been made into a large classroom while the rest of the building and fellowship hall had been remodeled and was fresh and clean. This meant that there were plenty of classrooms and also a fine fellowship hall in the basement.

But what made us love this church were the people. The twelve elders were godly men of faith and character. Each of them could make a long story by themselves of whom and what they were. Their names included Bernard Carr, Clarence Lambdin, John Gordon, Chester Horn, Tom Gordon, Harley Hudson, Gerald Ringo, Fred Klarman, Ed Rauch, Tom Piatt, Les Allison and Ora Winters.

The church had a fine grand piano, an Allen organ and many talented musicians. They already had great music and Margaret added her skills as well. When it was time to preach the congregation had been well prepared for the sermons. The church was full of wonderful Christians.

Adith Poole

What a pleasure it was to meet Adith Poole, who taught Sunday school. I had the chance to visit with Adith before very many weeks passed. She came into my office and gave me a history of the church.

More than 125 years before, the church began in this small village, by a ladies Bible study group that met to study the Scriptures and pray that a church could be founded in their community.

The church was in Shelby County, but to the west of Highway 51 that ran north and south through the middle of town, was Christian County. The town was half in each of the two counties. We jokingly said that Moweaqua was half Christian since one half of it was in Christian County.

Christian County had gotten its name from a revival meeting held west of town. It was led by one of the early Restoration Christian Church evangelists, possibly Alexander Campbell or Barton W. Stone. No one seemed to know which preacher it was for sure.

Adith told how the ladies eventually found a preacher to come lead their group and the result was Moweaqua Christian Church. She heard the gospel as a small girl there and was baptized when she was about 12 years old.

She said she began to teach Sunday school at age 15 and had taught there ever since. She was now almost eighty. Adith never married but went to college and became a public school teacher. She insisted that her public teaching was really just additional Christian training that she gave the students in the Moweaqua School system.

It was no surprise to learn that the local school board was made up of five members from the church, while the high school principal was an elder and the grade school principal was a deacon at the church. Two thirds of the teachers of both schools were members of the church. More will be said later about this. Needless to say this school system was the best our children ever attended and probably one of the reasons all of them are so successful today.

Now back to Adith. She came into my office on another day and said she thought it was time for her to retire from teaching her class. She said, "I am now 77 years old and I just feel tired most of the time." I sorrowfully agreed she had earned the right to retire.

She did retire from teaching, and six weeks later I had her funeral which was huge with many of the students she had taught coming to pay their respects. She just may have been the most influential person to have ever been a member of the church, or to have lived in the community. There were many tears shed the day of her funeral as we lovingly laid her to rest in the local cemetery.

What About a Revival Meeting?

Some of the church's large membership had been absent due to discouragement before our arrival. The elders thought that if we began our ministry with a brief revival meeting it might bring these people back to church.

Even though we were still settling in, the elders decided that I should preach this revival. I suggested to the elders that it would be helpful if we had a great song evangelist to help bring in people. We decided to try to get Roger Bankson for this purpose. He and I had worked together in several evangelistic meetings successfully.

Since Roger lived in Missouri, it was not too long a drive to central Illinois, and we set the time for the meeting when he was free to come. This was before the fall school opening for Margaret and me. I had the sermons all prepared that I had used in several other recent revival meetings.

The meeting began on Sunday morning and ran through the following Sunday night with a rest night Saturday. Roger came and asked where he could set up his display of recordings of his music for sale. Roger was one of the top soloists in the country. He could, all by himself, fill the building to overflowing with people wanting to hear him sing.

I asked Wayne, Evelyn's husband, the chairman of the Deacons, where we could set up Roger's display of recordings. He informed me that it was the practice of the church to never sell anything in the church building, "It was to be a place of prayer and not to be a place of merchandising." I told Roger and a look of dismay spread across his face, but he did not comment.

Nothing more was said that Saturday evening and we settled him into the guest room of the old parsonage. We enjoyed an evening meal together and went to bed early in anticipation of a busy week beginning the next morning.

Who Was That at the Door?

Roger and I were greeting people as they came in through the double glass entry doors. About twenty minutes before time to begin a large, shiny-black limo pulled up in front of the doors and a man dressed in a black tuxedo, white shirt and black bow tie got out and came in. He asked me where Roger Bankson was; I pointed to him. He walked up to Roger and pulled open Roger's suit coat and put two brand new $100 bills in his suit pocket.

The man turned and left, got in the limo, and it drove off. Roger, with a confused look on his face, asked me who that was who put the money in his pocket. He wiped a tear from his eye. I asked one of the elders standing nearby if he recognized the man and the limo. He said he had never seen the man, nor the limo, before. Others standing near said they did not see a man come in, or a black limo pull up, although they should have been able to see both. We all stood there sort of puzzled. The elder, and Roger and I, clearly saw the limo, the man and his actions.

Roger then, with tears in his eyes, told us the rest of the story. Roger had a wife and five boys at home. He said he had not been very busy with his singing ministry lately and had left his wife at home broke, with hardly anything left to eat in the house. He told her not to worry as he would sell lots of recordings on Sunday and would wire her money on Monday morning so she would have food for the children.

Roger explained that Saturday evening he got on his knees by the bed and beseeched God to help him care for his wife and children. We asked people at the church and later in the community and no one had ever seen the big, black limo, nor heard of the man in the tuxedo.

What do you think? Just who were those men in the limo? Was God on the scene helping Roger like He had helped me play a great game of golf back in Utah with the backslidden, arrogant, and boastful preacher? Could these have been angels? Roger and I were convinced they were (Hebrews 1:14).

Hearing the story of Roger's need, the elders agreed that Roger could set up his recordings for sale in the living room of the parsonage. We had a great revival and each evening after the services our house was filled with people fellowshipping, enjoying each other, and buying Roger's recordings.

A Sad Day for the Banksons

Roger's fame spread across central Illinois. Not long after our meeting in Moweaqua, he was invited to provide the music for a large rally held at a campground in southern Illinois. It was to be Friday evening through Sunday evening. Of course the crowds were enormous because there were healthy churches all over the area because of the fruitful ministry of Lincoln Christian College and Seminary.

By this time Roger and I had become close friends, almost like brothers. He called and told me this sad story. He said that since the rally was short he had brought along his wife Cheryl and his five boys for sort of a mini vacation.

After church on Sunday morning one of the attending families invited them to have lunch at a nearby small town restaurant. The Banksons gladly accepted. They enjoyed some fine home cooked southern Illinois type of food.

Roger and Cheryl had parked their van across the street from the restaurant and walked across the street to the restaurant as there was no parking nearer. When they were leaving the restaurant their youngest son, four years old, ran out between two parked cars into the street and was run over by a large grain truck that was going plenty fast on the two lane road through this small town.

Little Frankie was crushed. Roger said, "I grabbed him up in my arms and he cried out and breathed his last while I wept." Roger was sharing his grief with me. He is tender hearted and one of the most truly godly men I've ever known.

I asked, "Roger, you didn't go on with the program that evening, did you?" He replied, "Of course I did Charles, if the message we preach and sing about is true, I have something to sing about. If it isn't true then let's give up this farce. Yes, Charles, I sang through my tears and grief. God was honored and my and Cheryl's grief began to be assuaged."

For years we continued to work together in evangelism across America. Some of the meetings bore fruit for years afterwards. At one revival everyone in the church, except for the preacher and elders, responded to the invitation to either accept Christ or renew their vows to Jesus. Roger's singing was powerful evangelism.

The Youth Ministers in Moweaqua

The church already had a children's minister, Trudy Graham. She was a pretty and vivacious young lady who had recently graduated from Ozark Christian College in Joplin, Missouri. Her responsibilities were to oversee the youth Sunday school, Sunday evening youth meetings and Wednesday evening children's programs.

Trudy was doing a very fine job and I soon learned that she was hard working and creative. The children's programs were in good hands. Her office was just down the hall from mine and she often stopped by my office to discuss what she was hoping to do. This made for a harmonious working relationship between us.

She was single and I noticed that a young man began to attend church and hang around Trudy's office. I was saddened, but not surprised, to learn that they were engaged and soon to marry. I was not sad because of her marriage but the fear of the loss of her on staff. Just a few months after we came she offered her resignation as she was married and moving to another city with her new husband.

Trudy's Replacement

I was glad when the elders appointed a committee to find a new youth minister. I was super busy with school by this time and was settled into preaching and teaching. I did not even meet with the search committee until they brought in a young man to be interviewed. His name was Terry Mauer.

Terry graduated from Cincinnati Bible College with a degree in youth ministry. He had a lovely wife, Debbie, who was expecting their first child. After meeting Terry it appeared to me that the committee had come up with a fine young man.

We hired him and he moved into Trudy's old office and thus begun what became a warm working relationship. But it soon became clear that Terry had a few rough edges.

The first thing I noticed was his rather colorful speech. One of his favorite expressions was, "Oh, C&%p in the Morning." After the first few times I heard him say this I asked him if he knew what "C&%p" was. He said he had no idea. I told him it was what cows did on the barn floor and in the barnyard. He replied, "Oh no, you got to be kidding me!" He then replied that he had never been to a farm. He was embarrassed that no one had ever told him what that word meant as he had been saying it for years. He thought it just meant something was not too great or worthless.

One day I was working on translating some of the Psalms from Hebrew into English. Terry came in with three glasses of orange juice, two in his hands and one he held by the rim of the paper cup in his teeth. He walked up to my desk where I was working and said, "I brought you a glass of juice." When he said this he lost the cup he held in his teeth and the juice spilled all over my Hebrew Bible and notes. We got the Bibles cleaned up but the notes were a total loss. I had to begin over again.

Together Terry and I would often make hospital calls in Decatur. Seeing people along the street he referred to their sizes and shapes as, "thunder belly, thunder buns or thunder thighs." I could mention several other rather descriptive terms that probably did not suit a minister's vocabulary. We had a cordial conversation about what kind of language was befitting a minister of Christ. He was receptive and soon developed more socially acceptable and a bit less colorful vocabulary.

Terry grew into a fine church leader and served the Moweaqua church the rest of his life. A few years into his ministry he contacted a bad case of the flu and it destroyed his heart.

He was fortunate to get a heart transplant and lived another 20 years before dying rather young. The last I knew his wife, Debbie, had remained in Moweaqua where she raised their children.

One day we stopped for lunch at a fish restaurant in Decatur after visiting the hospital. We both ordered a shrimp basket lunch with fries. I noticed that he was eating the shrimp tails and all. He would sort of crunch them down with a look of discomfort on his face. I explained that the tails were not to be eaten.

The whole church and I dearly loved Terry. He was an excellent youth minister. He lived many years afterwards, but did die young because of his heart problems. I think of Terry and Debbie with love and fondness. One of the benefits of being a preacher is working with such fine and dedicated people.

The First Visit to the Seminary

We arrived in the late spring in Moweaqua and before we had a chance to settle into our work at the church, we decided to visit the campus at Lincoln Christian College. School was to begin in August. We were anxious to visit the campus since we hadn't seen it yet. We took a Monday to go to Lincoln and visit the school.

We were introduced to President Leon Appel, other administrators and several of the faculty. They were an impressive group. We already knew Dr. Shaw and Dr. Randall. But to meet men like John Ralls, Dr. Robert Wilson, and Dr. James Strauss and many others had left us super impressed. My first impression of Dr. James Strauss was that no human could be that smart.

The campus was also impressive. There were two main classroom buildings, one very large one for Lincoln Christian College and the other, somewhat smaller, for Lincoln Christian Seminary. There was a large cafeteria and sports complex and gymnasium. The library was a separate large building with over 127,000 selected volumes.

But the building that impressed us most was the Phillips Memorial classroom and chapel building. It had been built and donated by the Phillips family. The chapel would seat 3,500 and had a huge pipe organ. It is just like the one the Mormon Church has in their large chapel on Temple Square in Salt Lake City.

Margaret was going to be a music major and would often get to play this beast of an organ. She said it was like having a tiger by the tail. At full volume it would make the walls and windows vibrate. Once, while playing for a packed house rally there, she got a resounding standing ovation that went on and on.

The campus was hundreds of acres and one street across the campus was called "Campus Drive." It was where many of the administrators and professor families lived. There were also fine dormitories and also a large married student housing complex. Sometimes I stayed in the dormitory on Tuesday nights so I did not have to drive back and forth from Moweaqua. This was especially true when I had to do research in the library.

President Appel treated me like a long-lost younger brother when he learned that we both had been led to the Lord by the same preacher, Archie J. Word, who had also had a part in recruiting both of us to ministry.

We were greatly saddened by President Appel's sudden death by a heart attack the very next year. His hearty greeting, warm smile, and helpful service were missed by all. He was up north fishing and had a massive heart attack. He was so far from medical help that he died before they could get him to medical care.

We were now ready to begin driving the fifty-one miles from Moweaqua to Lincoln in just a few weeks when school began. I would attend two days a week, Tuesday and Wednesdays, and Margaret four days a week, Tuesday through Friday. Two days a week we drove together and the other days she drove herself. We put lots of miles on our cars during those three-and-one-half years.

Now Back in Moweaqua

Bernard

Many of the people in the church were extraordinary. One of these was Bernard Carr, one of the elders. He was older but still farming his large acreage, as well as a neighboring ranch, that he farmed for a widow lady. He and I were visiting her in the hospital one day, where she was recovering from surgery, when Bernard asked her, "Betty, what do you always think of when you think of me?" She replied, "You always talk way too loud!" She was right.

Because he did such a great job farming her ranch, she decided to buy him the finest new Buick car available for his birthday. It was a classic beauty of which he was justifiably proud.

He insisted that I drive it and we drove out towards Lake Shelbyville. On our way back a skunk ran out in the road ahead of us and I did all I could to miss the skunk without wrecking his fine new Buick. I said to Bernard, "I think I missed him." He replied, "Nope—you got him!"

When we got out of his fine new car he was right. If I did miss him, he had not missed us. His new car stunk to high heaven. I think it had to sit outside for a few days, because his wife, Pearl, would not let him keep it in the garage.

The Ambulance Drivers

Since the church only paid me as a part-time preacher ($650 monthly), a few extra dollars were always welcomed. The local ambulance service was run by the local mortuary. The owner of the mortuary and ambulance service was a member of the church and talked me into being one of the on-call drivers (calls were infrequent). I found that Bernard was the other driver. I learned more about him rather quickly, one thing was that, even though he was rather old, he was a speed demon!

It was about three blocks from the church parsonage to the ambulance. It was also about the same distance from Bernard's house. When we got calls they were most often at night. The first call came and I dressed rather quickly and hurried to the garage. Bernard was there behind the wheel and had the ambulance running to warm up.

Wow, was I in for a scary ride. He loved tragedy and also loved driving the powerful machine as fast as it would go. We were running out through the countryside through the corn fields. There were roads every mile running crisscross. We could not see traffic on the cross roads because the corn was too tall.

At each crossroads there was a rise where the roads crossed. We were airborne at each one and I was in the rear trying to keep the person, dead or alive, secure while not bouncing off of the ceiling of the ambulance myself. It was difficult for me to be secure while I sat next to the person belted into the bed.

Then we came into town, and that was when I really got scared. Bernard would run the siren at full blast and take the traffic lights at 70 or more miles per hour in thirty-five mile zones, as we raced to the hospital. I learned a new level of intercessory prayer.

When the third call came, I was prepared. I had a chair next to my bed with pants, zip up boots and a sweater that I could pull on as I ran flat out towards the ambulance. I got there, and a few minutes later, Bernard came in huffing and puffing and said, "How did you beat me here?" He had wanted to drive. I did not explain that fear made me run really fast. Everyone was safer from then on because he never beat me to the ambulance again.

Often we were called out in the middle of the night to collect a cadaver or a critically ill person to rush to the hospital in Decatur about 25 miles away. We ran all over the county helping sick or dying people.

One night we ended up at a car wreck. Five young men were out partying. They were pretty stewed. They were traveling at high speed up Highway 51 and tried to pass a car and hit the rear dual wheels of a heavily loaded semi-trailer coming towards them. It blew out three of the four rear semi-trailer tires.

All five fellows flew out the front windshield of the car and were spread all over the road. One's head was split open with his brains showing. Others had broken bones, but being totally drunk all five somehow survived, but I suspect they were never ever the same. We did get them to the hospital without any of them dying. It still seems impossible that the one young man lived.

A television crew showed up and got a picture of me working over the man with the open skull. The news said one of the victims was Charles Crane and our phone rang most of the night, with one call after the other, asking if I was going to live.

Through these outings Bernard and I became close and loving friends. We had many good times together in ministry and helping the sick and dying. Sometimes the people were already dead when we got to them.

Back at the Seminary

On our next visit to Lincoln Christian College and Seminary, I was introduced to Dr. and Mrs. Earl Hargrove. Earl was the founding president of both of the colleges. His wife, Jessie, was an immediate hit with me as my mother's name was Jessie and she reminded me of my mother.

I asked about the beginning of the school and here is what Dr. Hargrove told me. "I was the preacher of the Lincoln Christian Church and the church was doing fine. We were growing and there were regular conversions. But the rest of the State of Illinois was in serious spiritual trouble. There were about 120 Christian churches but they often lacked good leadership and when the pulpits were vacant they could not find well-trained preachers. "

"I began to pray about this problem and discussed it with a couple of my preacher friends—Charles Mills and Edward Tesh. We agreed that we needed a good Bible college in central Illinois to train a new wave of preachers to lead the churches and evangelize the Midwest. We agreed to start such a program and did so in the Lincoln Christian Church building. We called this the 'Lincoln Bible Institute.'"

Dr. Hargrove had preached the opening chapel sermon that he called, "The Preachers Are Coming." During the sermon he said in a loud voice, "The preachers are coming, the preachers are coming!"

This famous and great sermon was so popular that he preached it again at the beginning of school each fall. In fact, I heard him preach this sermon my first year at Seminary. It was an incredibly powerful message even though by that time it had been given many times and now was preached by a very old man.

Dr. Hargrove told me that day in his home, "Today there are over 600 Christian churches in Illinois and most all are healthy and growing. In addition, there are preachers across America and in many foreign countries that have graduated from the college and seminary."

Still today Lincoln Christian University and Seminary is a shining light for the gospel across the world. Dr. Hargrove and Jessie have been dead many years now but their influence still continues all over our world.

Back In Moweaqua

That afternoon when we arrived back in town, Margaret suggested that she was hungry and wanted to stop at the only restaurant in town. It was called "Wendall's." It was one of the nicest and prettiest buildings in town and the only true restaurant. There were no fast food places. We stopped and were warmly greeted by the owners.

Ralph and Berdella Wendall owned the restaurant and we found that they were members of the church that we had not personally met yet. Ralph was a master at making delicious pies and Berdella, his wife, knew how to make great home-style food. They were open all day and it was the watering hole for many prosperous farmers in the area. Each morning half of the place was filled with farmers eating breakfast and telling each other yarns.

We met the Wendalls and they insisted that our lunch was on them that day. We were often beneficiaries of their generosity. It was not long before we met Katherine, their waitress, who helped in many capacities. There were others who worked there but only the Wendalls and Katherine remain fixed in my mind.

I would have forgotten Katherine many years ago except for one outstanding trait. She professed to hate making milkshakes. If you ordered a milkshake she would begin to complain and voice her objection. We soon learned that she was just having fun with the customers and she didn't really object; but she would have all sorts of excuses why she didn't like to make them. When she saw our children coming she would begin to make a fuss and the kids learned to enter into the fun by ordering milkshakes. She sold lots of milkshakes.

We became great friends with the whole staff and ended up enjoying their cooking skills in the restaurant and at their home as well when we were invited there.

One evening while we were at the Wendalls' home a serious thunder and lightning storm came up. I worried about our T.V. and electrical things being in danger. Ralph suggested that I go unplug some of them and he would do the same at his house. If you have lived in this area you know how ferocious these storms can be.

I asked son Steve to ride home with me to help unplug things. We started up the street when a great bolt of lightning struck the ground about 100 yards up the street and a huge ball of electricity and fire came rolling down the street towards us. Steve dove under the dash and I braked. Just as the white glowing ball came to the car it dispersed into sparks shooting out from the ball then it all disappeared with a mighty clap of thunder.

White Medicine

It is hard to imagine a more-warm and welcoming village than Moweaqua. An evening routine was to ride bikes around town. Central Illinois is as flat as a kitchen table. One native said it is wonderful there as you cannot see a mountain anywhere. In fact it was so level one could see grain elevators in nearby towns. This made bike riding easy and fun. I had a bike and began to enjoy this evening activity when one evening I was stopped and asked to go to one of the member's home.

They wanted me to get Margaret and the kids and come back for "White Medicine." I asked what that was and they said it was homemade ice cream. I collected the family and we learned another thing about our new home. The people of the community were loving and generous with all of us; even those who were not members of the church treated us kindly. It was a happy and wholesome place. It was quite clear that the church had helped make this a wonderful place to live.

It was common to ride around town in the evening looking for where "White Medicine" was being made and served. Since we had a freezer to make homemade ice cream we also got into the white medicine culture.

Look out for Bernard!

One night while out riding my bike, I came across Bernard Carr riding his bike. He was my ambulance buddy. He challenged me to a race on our bikes. You remember how he liked speed. I was in for a great challenge and he shot ahead of me and ended up almost crashing into me when I finally passed him. We laughed and had a glorious time.

Friday Evening Fun

One of the fine church families, Clarence and Rhea Lambdin, were some of the very first to make us welcome in Illinois. They offered their assistance with church work doing what they could to help us with our extra busy schedules. They were always godly and faithful Christians helping our young family.

Clarence noticed that I had our small R.V. parked next to the driveway near the old parsonage and asked if I would like to have a place to park it in out of the weather. I replied, "Of course I would like that."

He suggested that I bring it out to his place, a few miles out of town and park it in a corn bin that was empty. It was just the right size and I was so happy to have it in a dry and secure place. There were remnants of corn, dust and remains of corn cobs, but it was dry and secure.

Later Clarence bought it from me as I was too busy to use it and all it did was sit at his place. He paid a very generous price which helped us meet educational expenses.

One Sunday Clarence and Rhea invited us to dinner at their place after church and introduced us to their daughter Rhonda and son-in-law Dean Jones. I was super impressed as Rhonda must have been in the top three most beautiful women in all of Illinois. Dean was a godly and handsome prince of a man.

I learned that Rhonda could also sing beautifully, and she often did at the church. They lived a few miles south of Moweaqua where Dean owned a race track, Motion Raceway. It happened to be one of the top-rated racetracks in America. Before the afternoon was over Dean had given me an annual entrance pass to all events at Motion Raceway, even the mechanical pits. This pass was good for our whole family and also our friends.

It was only about an eight-mile drive to the track; my first impression on arriving there was WOW, what a place! It was the number one race track-drag strip in the Midwest. Racers came from all over America to compete there.

Needless to say, Doug, Steve, and I spent many evenings there watching the races. Carol Beth went with us on many occasions. I even took Margaret a few times, but the noise was a bit too much for her sensitive ears. We had free entrance to all events and even the pits where mechanics worked on their cars.

We saw many of the most famous racers in America that came to compete, men like Captain Scotty, the Snake and the Mongoose, and many others whose names escape me.

I remember Captain Scotty came with his go-cart racer. It was powered by a hydrogen-peroxide jet engine or some such thing. When he raced, it made a sound like a giant jet engine. He did the quarter mile at 225 miles an hour in what looked like a small child's go cart.

There were all shapes and kinds of racers. Some looked like standard cars or pickups. Others were rails, with long bodies, big tires on the rear, engine in the middle and smaller nose and tires out front. These would make a terrible racket and burn out their tires a few times before racing to get the tires sticky for maximum traction. Fire would shoot out of their exhausts and blue smoke from their spinning tires.

There were two lanes, side by side, where a pair could race. Between the lanes was what was called a "Christmas Tree"; it was a pole of lights from top to bottom. The top lights, all but the bottom one, were yellow/orange with the bottom light green. When it was time to race the lights would count down and when green came on, off shot the vehicles.

All sorts of things then happened. One time the car burned out its tires, got settled in exactly the right spot to race and when the light turned green with a mighty roar the car jumped and parts spewed out from under the car in all directions and with a mighty shudder it just sat where it was, with smoke ascending skyward.

On several other occasions all sorts of things happened, blown tires, awful wrecks, some rolled over, some spun out and hit the guard rails, some somersaulted end for end, other times parts flew off, and on a few occasions the two cars ran into each other. But most often it was a race with a winner earning money or points for national competition.

With our busy schedule this provided an interlude from serious things. This was a time of serious bonding in our small family. It was something that Doug, Steve, and I enjoyed together and was the beginning of many future wonderful times together around cars, motorcycles, airplanes, and sporting events.

Yes, a preacher's life needs to be filled with hard work, but it also is often filled with so many wonderful experiences that other professions seldom provide. There are social events, worldwide travel, meeting important people, and helping those in times of crisis. Seldom are their lives boring, but often the preacher and family are in the middle of important events. Some are local and sometimes nationwide or worldwide. If you want a life of adventure, you should consider becoming a preacher of the gospel!

Raising Children in a Christian Community

It was not long before it became apparent how important the Christian community was for our children, Carol, Doug, and Steve. It was a safe place for them. We did not worry about them riding their bikes around town nor for them to hang out with their friends. Later we learned there were a few things we might have worried about if we had known.

Lawn Mowing

Doug and Steve were both hard workers and began to mow lawns. I had brought my lawn mower, a 22-inch Briggs and Stratton push mower, from Salt Lake City. Doug asked if he could use it to mow a few lawns. In a few weeks he and Steve were mowing 27 lawns. Grass really grew fast in this town. In the summer there was plenty of rain and the hot humid weather. Sometimes the lawns had to be mowed more often than once a week.

I would see Doug or Steve hook up the old mower behind their bicycles with a short chain with a simple combination lock on it. They would ride off down the street with the mower swaying back and forth behind them. Later they would return thirsty and covered with sweat.

I never checked just how much money they made, but I later learned that they did very well. Both had good sense with money and it came in handy for them later. People commented about what a good job they did with their work.

Doug the Trader

Doug began to display special skill in "horse trading." We had given him a small gas powered airplane with a Cox gas engine on it for his birthday. After a couple of flights with it, all that was left was the engine. He had mounted it on a two by four and would run it occasionally. Somehow the propeller had survived the crashes.

One day Doug asked if he could trade it for a Citizen Band radio. That worried me as I could only imagine what a few boys might talk about on the air waves in a small town where many other people had similar radios. I told him he could trade if he promised not to use it.

A few days later he asked if he could trade the radio for a revolver. I looked at the gun and was even more worried. I told him he could trade if it was agreed that he would not buy or keep ammunition for it at the house, or in his possession. I would buy some bullets and we would go shoot it when he wanted.

The gun only lasted for a couple of weeks before he asked if he could trade the revolver for two broken down motorcycles. I went to see them and said to myself that neither would ever run again. With a sigh of relief I agreed, and was glad to see the revolver gone.

We hauled the two old trail bikes home and later that day he had one running and wanted to take it out to the Shewmakers' farm where he could ride it and we did. And later that week he had both running and all spruced up looking pretty.

A few days later he wanted to know if he could sell both of them for $175. This skill, along with his lawn mowing, other jobs and his saving what he earned made it possible for him to buy a brand new Toyota SR 5, extra cab, pickup when he was a junior in high school.

A Young Preacher Goes to Seminary

I still remember the two boys pulling the old mower behind their bikes down the street to mow lawns. They pulled it so far that they wore the tires off until the tread was all gone down to the metal rims. We ended up having to buy a new mower.

The Biscayne

During this same period Doug came home one afternoon and asked if he could accept the gift of a 1958 Chevrolet Biscayne car from one of the members. Now things were getting pretty serious. We agreed that he could accept it if the Shewmakers would let him keep it out at their ranch. His favorite buddy was Brent Shewmaker. Brent's parents agreed and thought the boys could develop driving skills running it around the ranch.

So we got the old Biscayne and I drove it out to the ranch. A few weeks later Doug and Brent complained that when they ran it, smoke boiled out from under the hood and exhaust. I went out to inspect it and immediately found the problem. The engine was clear full of motor oil. When I put the dip stick in to check the oil level it was full clear up to the top of the stick.

I asked them what they had done to it. They told me that they checked the oil and found it low so decided to add oil from Brent's dad's farm oil barrel. The old oil was black and the new clean oil was clear. They kept adding oil. But, when they checked it, all they saw, was the old black oil down on the stick. They had filled the motor level full. It was a wonder it would run at all.

I drained out seven quarts before its level was correct. But that was a small issue.

This was during the period when the Dukes of Hazzard was on T.V. They had been watching the Dukes drive and jump their car, the General Lee. So Doug and Brent decided to see if they could jump a ditch back of one of the fields. They took Brent's dad's tractor that had a scoop on the front and made a ramp leading up to the ditch on one side.

They got back as far as they could and ran the Biscayne as fast as it would go. They hit the ramp at about sixty miles an hour and managed to jump the ditch. But when they landed, the poor old Biscayne was never the same again. It suffered a bent frame and none of the doors would open after that; the center of the car was about six inches lower to the ground than it was before.

Since none of the doors would open, they had to adopt the policy of the Dukes of Hazzard of climbing in and out of the windows. Finally the poor old Chevy had to be taken to the junk yard. We and the Shewmakers rested easier after that.

Public School

The three children were so blessed by the public school. The administration, as well as the teachers, were models of Christian character and committed to Christ and America. The classes were founded on Christian principles and helped to give them a foundation in great public civic principles.

Carol Scroggins was the grade school principal and a deacon at the Christian Church. His wife, Judy, was a beautiful and helpful wife. They and their children were active in the church. Doug and Steve were in grade school under his leadership.

Ed Rauch was the high school principal and he was an elder in the church. Both of these men were the kind of role models parents would want to teach and be examples for their children. Carol was in high school.

Doctor Pistorious

When putting the R.V. in the Lambdin's corn bin I picked up "histoplasmosas" or however it is spelled. It was a bird-borne disease that affected my breathing and lungs. I showed up sick and one of the ladies in the church invited me to come see Doctor Pistorious.

I was there bright and early Monday morning and Hazel introduced me to the doctor. He welcomed me gladly, examined me, and determined what was wrong with me and personally gave me free the medications I was to take. When I asked to pay him for his service he said he would treat me and our whole family for free, even providing what medicines we would each require.

For the remainder of our time in Moweaqua we received the finest medical care from this very generous clinic. It was another way God blessed our lives and made it possible for both Margaret and me to earn degrees and end up only in debt for a total of $2,000. Thank you, Doctor Pistorious.

First Day in Class at Seminary

Finally we were enrolled in school, Margaret in the under-graduate college and I in the Seminary. We were in for several years of rigorous intellectual and spiritual disciplines.

One of the first classes I was required to take was called, "Introduction to Seminary Curriculum." This seventeen-week course examined each of the majors offered by the Seminary. The professors each taught a two-hour class that surveyed what was taught in their department. Some of the departments were Preaching, Old Testament, New Testament, Hebrew, Greek, Church History, Psychology, Philosophy, the Sixteenth-Century Reformation, the Restoration Movement history, Evangelism, Church Growth, Missions, and there were many other classes on New and Old Testament books, and so forth.

It became apparent this was no Sunday school program, but a place where some of the finest intellects had gathered to be sure the church had thoroughly prepared theologians. The professors included such people as Dr. Robert Wilson, Dr. James Strauss, Professor John Ralls, Charles Mills, Edward Tesh, and Dr. Wayne Shaw, along with many others. More will be said about the professors later.

Little Galilee Christian Assembly

About thirty miles north of Moweaqua was the area's Christian camping grounds. Being in central Illinois, the campgrounds were situated next to a large borrow pit that had been dug to get gravel and dirt for road building and making overpasses on a freeway nearby. In comparison to our campgrounds out west it was not much to behold. But there was this big hole in the ground that had filled with rain water that made sort of a makeshift lake.

This was to be a men's retreat sponsored by the Mid-state church planting men's group. I had been asked to speak. Bernard Carr and Harley Hudson, elders in Moweaqua, had taken note of my little travel trailer and talked me into having them go with me to the meeting and the three of us sleeping in the R.V. It was not such a good idea, I soon learned.

I was asked to speak to the men, which I did. It was another time of sweet fellowship with Christian men from across central Illinois. It amazed me to see such harmony, love of each other, and commitment to expanding the church in the surrounding communities.

After the evening events we retired and each had our own bed in the trailer, but the idea of sleep soon vanished. Both Bernard and Harley were the worst snorers I have ever heard. It was such an awful racket I finally got up and dressed and walked clear across the camp grounds and I could still hear the awful racket. It sounded like a barrel with someone drumming on the inside.

I later learned that Harley's wife Norma insisted that their bedrooms be at different ends of the house. She said that even with both doors closed she sometimes had to put a pillow over her head to sleep. (So much for warm brotherly Christian fellowship—well…maybe????)

Great Gas Mileage

The story about the night I tried to sleep in the same trailer with Bernard Carr and Harley Hudson sort of goes along with this next story. Since Harley worked for Caterpillar Company in Decatur, this story seems to fit here.

Another one of the deacons from the church also worked at Caterpillar and he told me this story that had happened at work. One of the many other employees bought a new, small, French car that was reputed to get great gas mileage.

He showed his new, shiny silver, four-door sedan car and bragged that it would get over 40 miles per gallon once it was broken in. This was during the gas shortage and he was super proud and bragged after each fill up how great his mileage was.

One of the supervisors got tired of hearing him brag about his mileage so he asked one of the men working under him to go out and add some gasoline to the car. He was soon getting over 50 mpg and really began to brag. So they added more gasoline and he finally was getting up to over 90 mpg and the dealer that sold it to him had him bring it in to be examined by someone from the manufacturer.

They could not discover anything too different about his car but had no answer for his super mileage. So the boss at Caterpillar sent the same man out with a siphon hose and they began to remove gasoline, just a little, so his mileage began to drop until it was only getting 20 mpg and then that dropped to about 10 mpg.

He returned to the dealership with his complaints about his new car. Together they began to smell a rat and investigation found the culprit. Then the man was super embarrassed and angry. Finally his car settled in to a steady mpg of around 40 which was normal.

One of the First Classes

Since Dr. Max Ward Randall had encouraged me to come to Seminary, the very first semester I signed up to take one of his mission classes. It was called, "Planting Indigenous Churches on the Mission Field." It was a wonderful class where I gained much valuable information on the subject.

Dr. Randall had planted mission works on three continents. The one that stood out most clearly in my mind was his work in Zimbabwe, Africa. He had gone to evangelize where the famous English missionary, David Livingstone, had done his work years before. There were still some remainders of the previous work but it was failing and Dr. Randall wanted to ply his skills in establishing the work with the indigenous people in charge of and leading the work forward toward a permanent future.

I clearly remembered Dr. Randall's class, and later taught some of his material in Zimbabwe on three different occasions for a month each time. On one of these trips we made a special effort to visit the site of David Livingstone and Dr. Randall's work. What did we find?

Getting to the place was no small challenge as it was very remote. We boarded a boat on Kariba Lake that was above the huge dam on the Zambezi River. This is the second largest man-made lake in the world. It is second in size only to the High Aswan Dam and lake on the Nile River in Egypt.

We were to travel up the lake for 220 miles with about 125 other people on the boat. This trip was to be overnight and we all were to sleep in a big covered veranda. There were chaise lounges with about one foot between them spread out in this huge space.

When it was time for bed, people began to undress and put on their sleeping clothes. This was all done somewhat modestly. We slept in the clothes we were wearing. We were anxious about trying to sleep in such unusual circumstances. But Margaret and I slept in lounges next to each other. Since we were exhausted we did sleep some.

The trip up the lake and river was like traveling through a zoo. There were all sorts of wildlife all along. We saw many elephants, hippopotamuses, zebras, big crocodiles, and many different types of birds, and even some water snakes.

Food was another matter. We were fed things that we had never eaten before. One stands out in my mind. They were called Kapenta fish, which were small sardine-like things, totally whole with nothing removed. These little Kapenta fish that we ate had been dipped in some sort of batter and then left in the sun until they dried out and were rather crisp. They had a mild fish taste and were sort of crispy and good tasting. Later when I saw how they were prepared I realized they had been covered with bugs and flies during the preparation process as they had been dipped in batter and left out in the sunlight for several days.

The next day we arrived at our destination which was at a French resort near where the mighty Zambezi River entered the lake. This was a totally remote place. There was no electricity in our rooms. They were sort of round huts. There was running well water for showers and for the toilets. The water was heated out-side in cement towers that had pipes running through the con-crete and places for a fire to be built to heat the concrete with the water pipes in it. We had lanterns for lighting in the huts.

We were to eat at the main building and we were in for a feast. The French restaurant served all sorts of things. We had beef, kudu, wart hog, flamingo, ostrich, bream and several other kinds of unknown fish, plus all sorts of vegetables and many tasty dishes.

When it was time for dessert we had all sorts of choices of French delights. They kept our drinks of tea, iced or hot, coffee, and sodas full. Margaret and I were joined by the Marshalls and Martins. I had agreed to pay for the six of us and with a generous tip it cost me $26 U.S. A working man in Zimbabwe at that time earned $25 a month.

The next morning I had a scratchy throat. I was to begin teaching in a couple of days and was to speak for 54 hours in three weeks. I didn't dare end up sick. Ivan Martin said there was a medical clinic out in the bush that might treat me.

We drove there and were greeted by a rather brash German lady doctor. She spoke English but was communicating with a nurse with rather uncomplimentary comments about us in German. I entered into the conversation with my limited knowledge of the German language, and she immediately apologized for her comments.

She examined me and prescribed a round of antibiotics. The bill for her services and the medicine came to $6 U.S. I had told the missionary if she came out with a needle to give me a shot I was going to run like crazy. I heard that they re-used their needles.

I clearly remember the day we finally came to the main mission location. The mission site was on a high bluff overlooking the mighty Zambezi River below. As we arrived there was a commotion going on and the people were in an uproar. One of the male residents was getting water from the river when he was killed and half eaten by a crocodile.

We visited the site of the church building and the Christian school. There was a K–12 school in session. They were singing Christian songs that we could recognize the tunes but not the Shona words. There were about 125 students and it was the center of the small community.

Graduates of Boise Bible College, Ivan and JoAnn Martin, were working in the area and told me there were now 220 Christian churches throughout this part of Zimbabwe. Dr. Randall's indigenous church planting skills had worked wonderfully there. The work was still flourishing.

A few days later I was speaking to about 250–300 African preachers who had traveled from many miles to come to the training sessions. Some had walked over 100 miles to attend. Some came barefoot until within sight of the meeting place when they put on their shoes. They could not afford to wear them out.

The teaching sessions began at 8 A.M. and continued until lunch break. They resumed at 2 P.M. The preachers were sitting on makeshift pews made out of a round cut off of a tree that had an eight inch wide plank nailed to it on which they sat. At 4 P.M. I asked if they wanted to take a break. The vote indicated everyone wanted to continue. (I was the one most needing the break.)

These sessions lasted all week. On Sunday the church was packed beyond capacity. I preached and did not give an invitation because I feared some would respond just because an American was preaching. I did not want them to respond unless they were coming to Jesus, not to me. The presider who was called "Sixpence" (Can you imagine naming your boy Fifty Cents?) took over and he offered an invitation. So many people came to be baptized that they lined up clear around the large auditorium.

Sibonda, the preacher, baptized them and in a way I had never seen before. Sibonda had a voice like a bull horn. When the congregation was singing, he could out sing hundreds of people.

He got the person in the baptistery and made them get down on their knees in the water. He would then say the proper things and bend them back under the water. Just try getting on your knees and then bending back until under the water. The person was bent back like a spring. When he brought the person up out of the water they shot up like a released spring with water splashing everywhere. It was a joyous Lord's Day and people were rejoicing, singing, and praising God.

The preacher's clinic lasted two weeks and was followed by a revival meeting at The Hillside Chapel, an English-speaking church, nearby. This revival meeting was well attended and people were baptized there night after night. On the last night in Zimbabwe there was a large "Bri" or what we call a barbecue.

Hunting Safari

Dale Marshall, missionary and long-time friend, had learned that I had grown up hunting on our ranch and asked if I would like to go on an African hunting Safari. I had jumped at the chance.

One of the Christians from Hillside Chapel, Andy, was a hunting guide and agreed to take me hunting on our last full day in Zimbabwe. I asked if I could come to his home to check out the rifle I was to use to be sure I could fire it accurately.

At 5 A.M. he handed me the rifle. As I took it I found that it was identical to the rifle I had always used to hunt with back on our ranch at home. I asked how it was sighted in and he said it shot two inches high at 250 yards. I replied I did not need to shoot it but was ready to go hunt.

The guide asked if I had a choice of what to hunt and I replied that I would love to hunt Kudu. We traveled out to the wilderness, called the bush, and began to see all sorts of Kudu. He kept saying, those bulls are too small. We'll find some great ones.

Finally we came to a huge meadow of thousands of acres and about 250–300 yards away were three great bull Kudus. I was riding in the pickup bed and he stopped and said, "Pick out the biggest and second biggest, shoot the biggest first and the smaller second." I asked, "Where should I shoot them?" He said, "A heart shot is best."

I pulled down on the biggest and fired one shot. The animal jumped in the air, ran about ten yards and collapsed. The other two set off at a dead run. I shot a second time and missed. I pulled down more carefully, shot again and the second largest hit the dirt and skidded to a stop.

Both Kudu were trophy animals, the largest horns measured 45 inches above the head and the smaller just a bit less. They estimated that the largest was 1,250 pounds and the smaller about 900. I asked our guide, Andy, what will be done with the meat? He told me that everything would be eaten, not a scrap would be wasted. The meat would be given to poor Christian families from the church. The horns were shipped to me and I still have them.

That evening at the Bri, our guide got up and addressed the about 75 guests. All month I had been razzed by the guide and several of his friends about Americans not being able shoot or to hit an animal, saying that they couldn't even hit an elephant with a gun if it was tied up in the field. All of this kidding had led to my praying earnestly that morning that I might shoot accurately.

He said, "Dr. C.C. (which is what they had learned to call me), is a shooter. I told him to heart shoot the Kudu and he shot the top off of the heart of the biggest and the bottom off of the heart of the smaller." Frankly I only had a general idea where the hearts were.

I got up and told them that I had prayed earnestly that I would shoot accurately just like I had also prayed that I would preach accurately. I suggested that the shooting was proof that God answers prayer.

This was another way God was blessing the young preacher with being able to go on an African safari for free. There are hundreds of ways God often blesses His servants, way beyond the average person. Preachers' lives are filled with extraordinary events seldom experienced by people in normal life.

Come Shoot Baboon

One of the farmers at the Bri, asked me if I would come out and hunt baboon on his ranch, saying he had 25,000 acres and the baboon ruined his crops. (He did not know that we were heading home the very next day.)

He explained that a baboon would walk through a field of corn, picking it. They would pick an ear and put it under one arm, pick another and put it under the other, walking clear through the field picking corn and only end up with two ears as they kept dropping ones they had already picked and placed under their arms.

He said, "Come hunt, I will supply a jeep, gun, ammunition, and $50 for each one you shoot." He said they were pretty smart and really hard to catch and kill. I told him I was heading back to America the next day.

I then asked him what it was like to shoot a baboon and he replied, "It is like shooting one of your cousins." Well, I have never shot a cousin, but thought I wasn't interested in killing baboons either.

Andy, the Guide

Andy had a smaller ranch, about 3,000 acres, but led hunting safaris, since he enjoyed hunting. The week before going hunting with him he had come to the missionaries' house at lunch time. We had a nice visit while we ate lunch.

The stories he told me were some of the most awesome tales I have ever heard. He showed me awful scars on his face and head. Andy said he was down at the Zambezi River getting water for their camp when a crocodile caught him. He said the beast had slapped him with its tail and caught his head in its mouth. He said that he always carried a hunting knife on his belt and managed to kill the crocodile before it drowned him in the river. He said he was honored as the only known person to survive a crocodile attack with his head in its mouth.

He went on to tell about being attacked by a large male lion. He was leading a hunt for lion and the hunter he was guiding shot a big male but only wounded it. As they tracked the wounded lion, it charged Andy and when he tried to shoot it, his gun jammed. He threw down his gun and when attacked he rammed his left arm down the lion's throat, clear into its stomach. He made a fist in the lion's stomach, who was now sort of incapacitated.

But now what to do? The hunter was not there right then and the only other person was his native assistant, "boy" who had never shot a gun. While fighting with the lion, Andy's boy helper was working frantically to unjam the gun and get it ready to fire. Andy was trying to give instructions.

Andy said his "boy" had never shot that gun and was to shoot the lion while his arm was in its mouth and down its throat. "I had two worries," Andy said, "the lion and having my arm shot off by someone that had never shot any gun before." He pulled back his shirt and showed me the wounds he had on his arm and shoulder. His "boy" did manage to kill the already wounded lion.

Six Months Later

Before this trip to Zimbabwe I had read a book entitled *Death in the Long Grass*. It told about all the wild animals and snakes in Africa. It told how there were many that were terribly dangerous, but the most dangerous of all were the Cape buffalo. They were so tough they were hard to kill. They were smart and if you wounded one of them they would stalk you and try to kill you if possible.

On one of our trips I had been confronted by five Cape buffalo. When coming over a ridge and seeing five of them with their heads down looking at me, I never ran faster in my life. But the missionary ahead of me was running even faster and he was pulling away and heading to jump into the Zambezi River with its crocodiles and hippopotamuses, not to mention bilharzia.

About six months after returning home from the Kudu hunt I received word that brother Andy had been killed on a hunt by a wounded Cape buffalo. Thank goodness Andy was a devout Christian.

Back in Moweaqua—Coins

My father, Claude C. Crane, died young, just after his 59th birthday. He and I had been exceptionally close all my life. After his death, my mother gave me a small metal Calumet baking soda can full of old coins. My father had put old and unusual U.S. coins in the can ever since he was a boy. I treasured these coins as they were one of the few things I had that had been my father's. I also still have a box of tools that he gave me that I still use. I treasure his small pocket Bible that is in my desk drawer.

Around my birthday each year, I had a practice of adding a few old U.S. coins to this collection. In Moweaqua there were two old bachelor brothers, Raymond and Rodger, who had never married. Their chief hobby in retirement was coin collecting. They traveled all over the Midwest to places where coins were being bought and sold.

Raymond found out about my small collection and wanted to see what I had. He and his brother came to the parsonage and I spread out the coins on the kitchen table. They told me that I had several quite valuable coins. They offered to help me add to this collection.

Roger suggested that I get a "type set book" to put my coins in and this would keep them safe and let me know what coins I needed to complete a set of every type of coin ever minted in the United States. They helped me find this book and it was clear that I needed many coins to complete this set. In addition they helped me get books for other types of coins so that I could collect every year they were minted. Such coins as Indian Head pennies they thought I should concentrate on. Eventually I had every year of Indian Head pennies.

The collection now had Flying Eagle pennies, half dimes, three-cent pieces, twenty-cent coins, copper/nickel pennies, large cents and various kinds of nickels, dimes, quarters, half and silver dollars. They helped me get nearly every type of coin that had ever been minted in America for circulation. Some type of coins I have every year they were minted. These coins were supplied to me at such a reasonable cost I could not refuse, even though we were sacrificing financially to attend college.

At the same time, I had begun to collect coins that related to biblical history. The collection begins with coins from Alexander the Great and Phillip of Macedon, his father. The collection dates from 330 B.C. to A.D. 1250 with many from New Testament times.

A Young Preacher Goes to Seminary

Some Great Seminary Classes

One class that will always stand out in my mind is the one taught by Dr. James Strauss. As already mentioned, my early impression of Dr. Strauss was that he had a huge ego problem, since no one could be as smart as he appeared. I was soon to learn how wrong my evaluation of him actually was. What appeared was only the tip of the iceberg, so to speak, of what he really knew and was.

The first class I took from him was called, "The Making of the Contemporary Mind." In this philosophy class, Dr. Strauss traced the thinking of the whole world and what was thought and believed from ancient Assyria until modern America. He stressed that there were just five people that had truly shaped the thinking of the world.

This class was attended by over 200 people and was held in a huge classroom in the marvelous chapel building. This wonderful building had been built by the Phillips family of oil company fame. The large room had blackboards on three of the four walls. In a two-hour class Dr. Strauss would write the blackboards full and usually in three or four different languages.

His classes were so dynamic, that try as I might, I was not sure of what he was talking about sometimes for several days, or weeks. But by taking notes and doing all I could to follow him, after a couple of weeks or more it all became clear. His teaching was masterful beyond description.

In this class he not only traced the thinking of the world but we also covered all twelve departments of the modern university and the thinking behind each discipline.

According to Dr. Strauss, each department of the University had been taken over by the "Progressive" idea. The progressive idea is a new way of saying "evolution." The idea is that given time and the efforts of mankind, everything can continue to improve and move on towards perfection. Unfortunately, the very opposite is too often true. Even with our best efforts everything has a tendency to run down.

Does anything that is just left to itself get better? Does your house just get better and better, your car, your carpets, clothes, or your yard? Even with our best efforts things continue to run down. Has music gotten better? Has art continued to get more beautiful? Could nature, left all alone, have produced the human heart, eye, or, baby? It takes huge creative power and effort to create.

Strauss discussed the two evidences of God laid out by the Apostle Paul in the first chapter of Romans. Paul suggests that there are two evidences of God that every human experiences. These two witnesses are the internal and the external evidence that there is a creator God. God manifests Himself internally in the human heart and brain. The external witness is seen in what has been created.

Atheism and Agnosticism

One lecture discussed the problems with these views. Strauss told us the word atheist came from a Greek word that means "no God." He explained that no human is smart enough to truly be an atheist. To know that there is no God one would have to almost be God themselves. Has any human checked all the evidences for God? This would mean reading all written records. Has anyone traveled over all the earth to know for sure there is no God? Possibly while traveling God moved and they missed Him. Atheism, Strauss taught, was a philosophical and intellectual absurdity.

He then lectured on agnosticism. He showed us that the word agnostic came from a Greek word "ah gnossco" literally meaning

"I don't know." This is a more reasonable view he said, but this just means that the person is unlearned. He suggested it could be translated "ignoramus." He suggested that the wise agnostic should begin to research the subject of God and that almost always those who did so with an open mind became believers.

Dr. Strauss then gave us powerful evidence for a creator God. It would take a small book to go into all the details of his powerful presentation. But this brings us to the next page in this narrative.

Jon Murray

For years I had served on the Continuation Committee for the North American Christian Convention. I was still on the committee during my seminary days. That year the North American Convention was being held in Seattle, Washington. I was in attendance.

When the committee met, just before the convention began, the president said we had an invitation for one of us to debate Madalyn Murray O'Hair's son Jon on a local TV station. (You may or may not remember Madalyn Murray but she was the one who got prayer taken out of our public school system.)

No one was willing to debate Jon. And even though there were many more qualified than I was, none seemed willing. I finally raised my hand and agreed to do so. The debate was set to take place on Friday at 10 A.M. as best I recall.

When I arrived at the TV studio, they explained that Jon was an atheist and wanted to debate whether there was a God or not. I began to breathe easier, remembering the wonderful material Dr. Strauss had presented to us in his seminary class. This information was still crystal clear in my mind. Jon was a big man who tended towards obesity. He spoke with a limited speech impediment.

Jon presented his case for there not being a God and that the world was the result of millions of years of evolution and fortuitous variations that led eventually to our world as we know it.

It was clear he did not know what he was talking about, but was repeating disproven ideas and theories.

When it was my turn to speak I asked Jon, "So you are sure you are an atheist?" I explained that the word atheist came from a Greek word "a-theos" that meant no God. He affirmed that he was sure of his being an atheist. I explained a bit more about the root of the word's meaning and if he were an atheist then he knew there was no God! He agreed that he knew and could prove this.

I said, "Then you must have done quite a bit of research if you believe you can prove there is no God. You have read the whole Library of Congress and other great libraries around the world because somewhere in them there might be evidence for God? I also assume you have read and studied the Bible from end to end."

"You must also be really well traveled, Jon, having been all over the earth, because evidence for God might be found somewhere in the world. Oh, Jon, you have to be omniscient also, for God might have been there just before you arrived and moved on. Just as Dr. Strauss had taught in class, for a person to be an atheist they would have to be almost God themselves. So Jon, for our discussion I am going to assume that you are really an agnostic, not an atheist."

"As an agnostic I see real hope for you, Jon. In my humble experience, when a person researches the matter of whether there is a God with an open mind, they almost always end up finding Him. Jon, I am going to pray for you that you will find the God your older brother has found. "

"Jon, search your heart; have you ever had the notion, or feeling, that there just might be a creator? Has it ever sort of been impressed on you that all this order and design around us may be pointing to a wise and beneficent designer creator? Jon, have you in all your extended research, taken time to study the Holy Bible? Jon, faith comes by hearing and hearing by the word of God."

At that time I did not know what had transpired in Jon's life to make him what he was. I did not know that he never knew his father or that his father had only been a boyfriend of his mother. That day I felt sorry for him as even the moderator suggested that he had not made much of a case for his lack of belief in God. The audience had often laughed at him. I left the studio thanking God for the chance I had to go to Seminary and have such good information available for ministry.

Since then I have learned how Jon's life turned out. It appears that he never did find God or faith in Jesus Christ. His full name was Jon Garth Murray and he lived from November 16, 1954 until September 29, 1995. He served as president of American Atheists, a non-governmental organization that lobbied for the separation of church and state. He was the second son of Madalyn Murray O'Hair, who was an activist that had founded American Atheists in 1963 and she had served as its first president.

Jon, Madalyn, and a niece, Robin, were all kidnapped and killed in San Antonio by David Roland Waters, a former employee of American Atheists. Waters committed these crimes with the help of two other men. Jon was only forty years old at the time of his death. How disappointing and fruitless his life had been.

Looking back, it grieves me that the course of these events was not changed by the debate with Jon while he was still young and impressionable. As with all of our lives, when not subjected to the Lordship of Jesus Christ, the end is always tragic. So much harm has been done by people who have never truly taken time to think through their positions. How sad were the lives of Jon, his mother and his family. Finally at age 40 he was called to meet his maker and receive the reward of an ill-spent life. Five seconds after death there are no atheists or agnostics.

Not Much Evangelistic Opportunity

The small town of Moweaqua was such a desirable place to live, very few people ever moved away. It was sort of a bedroom community to house people that worked for Caterpillar Corporation in Decatur, which was about 25 miles to the north.

Occasionally someone died, which left an empty house. Very rarely someone would build a new house. Since the town only had 1,400–1,500 people and the Christian Church had 800 members and there were five other churches in town, the opportunities for evangelism were quite limited. Children from church families were sometimes baptized but there were a few holdouts against Christianity in the community.

It wasn't that there was no evangelism, since during the three-and-one-half years we were there a total of 87 people were baptized. These were primarily children from Christian families, some were people attending church who had never been baptized, and a few were from those in the community who were not Christians and had not been attending church.

One of these holdouts was Herb Jackson. Herb's wife, Denise, was a faithful member who worked hard teaching Sunday school and was a great help during Daily Vacation Bible School.

Herb was friendly but said he was too busy with his large ranch and all the work associated with it that he didn't have time to waste sitting around at church.

I had chosen Jack Dial as a person to disciple. When I did church work, Jack often went with me. On some occasions he visited people in the hospital with me. On the rare occasion that someone new moved to town we visited them together. I took him with me when visiting single women; sometimes we ate breakfast or lunch together just for fellowship.

Jack was a fine Christian man and his cute little wife, Millie, was always fun to be around when the four of us, including Margaret, fellowshipped together. Anyway, Jack and I had tried our best to interest Herb in the gospel but with negative results.

Herb Jackson Hospitalized

One day, while in class at Seminary, one of the secretaries came to me with a note that I needed to stop at the hospital on my way from Lincoln back to Moweaqua. I had to drive right past the hospital on the way home. The note said it was necessary to stop and see Herb Jackson.

I stopped at the hospital and learned Herb was in intensive care on the fourth floor. I went to his cubicle and found that Herb had suffered a tragic accident, having caught his coveralls in the power take off on his tractor and it had torn off his right leg at the knee. He had been rushed to the hospital and with surgery had survived, but he had lost his leg from the knee down. I was heartbroken about his accident.

As I approached him in intensive care, in his cubicle, his doctor and a nurse were by his bedside. Herb was having the most awful hiccups imaginable, literally making his whole bed jerk back and forth.

When I approached, Denise introduced me to the doctor as "Pastor Crane"; the doctor said he was so glad I came. He said, "We have done everything medical science knows to do to stop Herb's hiccups. Nothing has worked—would you pray for him?" I asked that we each lay our hands on Herb and together unite in prayer for him. When I said "Amen," Herb's hiccups stopped abruptly. He lay back exhausted and in terrible pain. At that time he could not visit with me.

I asked Denise about the details of the accident and suggested that if they needed my help to call. I gave her my phone number and excused myself. I then visited some other people from Moweaqua who were in the hospital and went on home exhausted, having been up since 4:30 A.M. We had a quiet evening and dinner at home and as usual I worked on my Seminary class work until midnight.

Exhausted, I fell into bed at about 12:15 and was instantly asleep. At 2 A.M. I was awakened by the incessant ringing of our phone. I instantly thought it was an ambulance call. I was surprised that the call was from the hospital in Decatur. It was the head nurse from intensive care; she said the doctor had asked her to call to see if I would come back to pray for Herb as his hiccups had returned.

I hastily dressed and rushed to Decatur and arrived about 2:45 A.M. Poor Herb was wracked with these awful hiccups. I came to his bed and laid both hands on him and prayed earnestly that his hiccups stop and not return. Soon his hiccups stopped and they never returned. A few days later Herb was sent home, but now his whole life was changed as he only had one good leg.

Jack and I returned to call on him and these calls soon became teaching sessions, and not long after, Jack and I baptized Herb into Christ his Lord. He had lost his leg but found his life. He has remained a faithful Christian. The story spread throughout the church and community. The whole town rejoiced in the joy that came out of tragedy. Moweaqua was basically a Christian community.

Another Day at the Hospital

Margaret and I often stopped at the hospital, so I could make my rounds on our way home from school at Lincoln. Two days a week we rode together to school. This day I made my rounds and discovered that next to the hospital, on Decatur Lake, they were having hydroplane races. Right through the middle of town was a river that had been dammed up that made a long and beautiful lake. This lake was right by the hospital.

Being really enthralled by the races, I suggested that Margaret take our car and go on to Moweaqua and get our three children and to bring them back to see the races; I would stay behind watching the races. She agreed and let me out where I had a good view. I promised that I would be right there where she let me out when she returned with the children.

Not long after she had departed, the sky to the west grew dark and then turned a greenish hue. This concerned me as I felt sure we were in for one of the awful summer lightning storms and maybe even a tornado. I was also concerned since there was no place to find shelter and to stand under a tree or shed was an invitation to get struck by lightning. I could not leave where I was since Margaret was to return to get me in a few minutes. The storm raged for the next three hours and Margaret did not return.

Soon it was raining torrentially. I was dressed in slacks, a dress shirt, a nice suit jacket and my zip-up Florsheim dress boots. It rained so hard that the road was flooded between Decatur and Moweaqua so that Margaret could not get back to me. In about two and one half hours it rained 7.5 inches while I was out in it. My boots were full of water and running over. I could have jumped in the lake and not been wetter.

It took several hours for the water to recede enough so she could come get me. Of course the races were cancelled. My clothes and shoes were pretty much ruined. What I wouldn't have given for a sturdy plastic umbrella. I didn't need to shower before going to bed that evening.

Transportation

While at Seminary a national energy crisis arose with escalating gasoline prices and even lines waiting at the service stations to purchase gasoline. The drive from Moweaqua to Lincoln was just over 50 miles. With a stop at the hospital in Decatur on our way home, it came to up towards 55 miles each way for a total of about 110 miles daily. This meant that transportation was an issue for us to get to and from college and Seminary. Not only was the fuel expensive, but the wear and tear on the car was too.

I attended Tuesday and Wednesday and Margaret attended Tuesday through Friday. Tuesday and Wednesday she rode with me and Thursday and Friday she had to drive herself. For the two semesters this amounted to about 15,000 miles of driving just going to school.

In those days cars needed more maintenance than they do today. Every 15–20,000 miles they needed a tune up; and not long after, a set of new tires. Sometimes they needed brakes or shocks. With the driving necessary for regular church work our main car was getting up to 25,000 miles of driving and with the increased cost of gasoline driving was one of our major expenses. I had no expense account at the church.

One of the administrators at the Seminary told me about a Chevrolet dealer in a nearby town who was a Christian and sold cars to ordained preachers at his absolute cost, well below what is called invoice. In addition, an ordained preacher in Illinois did not have to pay sales tax, an additional 7% savings on the price of purchase.

At the earliest opportunity I checked this out and found it was true. The total savings on a new car was about 30% below the normal purchase price. For this reason, we had a new Monte Carlo Chevrolet each year while in school. When the next year model came out, I sold the one I was driving, without spending one dollar on repairs, and purchased a new one.

I could sell the car I was driving at such a discounted price it would sell immediately. During the three years, we had a new car to drive each year and made a profit of over $800 with our only maintenance expense the price of oil changes. This extra money helped us pay for the expensive gasoline to drive all these extra miles. It was another way God helped supply our needs while going to school. It may have given more credence to Banker Ayar's rumor which he spread around that the new preacher was rich. That was not true. But nothing succeeds like success nor fails like failure. Having a new car also was not a burden either.

Other Seminary Classes

Advanced Introduction to New Testament

None of the classes at Seminary were easy, but two stand out as especially difficult. A three-hour class was called "Advanced Introduction to the New Testament." The professor was not much older than I. It was listed as a three-hour class, which meant we met for three hours a week for 17 weeks.

When the class syllabi are passed out, the normal response is to think this work load is impossible. I was more than shocked by what we were expected to do in one semester. The assigned reading was 4,750 pages which would be like reading the Bible through four times in 17 weeks. My response was WOW!

The next assignment was to write a 35-page paper on some approved subject. I approached the professor and asked if I could write my paper on "P-66." His response was, "Oh no, that is a late and unimportant document." I responded, "You mean the Bodmer II text of the Gospel of John from the year A.D. 140–200 is late and unimportant?" He replied, "You are going to have to enlighten me, as I do not know what you are talking about." I explained it was one of the most significant of our many ancient New Testament Greek manuscript copies.

I then explained that one of my hobbies was examining old biblical manuscripts and that summer I had been in Rome, Italy and seen the Bodmer II text and purchased a photocopy. It was in the Vatican Library in Rome and it was on display when we were there. I wanted to translate it from its Greek language into

English and to write a brief commentary on it. He was excited for me to do that. It was very enlightening, and one of the many things I learned was that I found that the word for faith in John is almost always a verb in its nearly 100 occurrences.

This class was really hard and required that I read many hours into the night all semester. I finished the class and it has really blessed my ministry ever since. Thank goodness that in my under-graduate training I had taken a class in speed reading, otherwise I would have never completed this class. I was the only student who did not have to ask for extra time to finish the reading.

But the Hardest Class of All Was Hebrew

Languages have always been one of my most difficult subjects. When I entered school at age six, I was not able to read. The eye tests showed that I could read every line on the eye chart clear across the room. They did not check my close vision, but assumed I had good vision.

I still could not read in the second grade and finally was taken out of school by my mother, Jessie, when I was in the third grade. She was sure she could teach me to read. After a couple of weeks of failure she took me to Dr. Crain, an eye specialist, who discovered that I was very far sighted and could not read even the largest headlines of the newspaper. He fitted me with glasses and in two weeks I was reading everything. I have read almost every night since.

Then, in high school, I wanted to learn the workings of the English language. I had taken English all four years, and not one teacher knew the basics of the English language. I had four years of poetry and literature. This was just after the Second World War and good teachers were hard to find in our small town.

In college, I found a professor who knew English and finally learned how English worked. I learned the parts of speech and how to diagram a sentence. But, by then I was not very confident with my ability to learn a language. I did take German in high school and can still sort of speak and read it. During college I did take two years of Greek.

Now, with much trepidation, I was enrolled to take Hebrew. The professor was John Ralls. He was a small man with intense eyes and a no-nonsense attitude. He told us right away that he could read all eleven Semitic languages as well as German and Greek. After the very first class I recognized that he was a genius.

I inquired about him and learned that as a boy he had been sickly and not able to engage in outdoor sports, but showed all the signs of genius. His parents had given him musical training, and he had also distinguished himself in school as a top scholar all the way to his doctoral work. He had little patience for anyone who could not memorize full pages of information in a few minutes.

His class members were off to learn Hebrew. In the first class, we learned that Hebrew has 22 consonants and 17 vowels. Whew, that sounded tough. The consonants looked really strange and the language was written from right to left, just the opposite of what I was used to. There were strange-looking symbols for each vowel. Their names sort of gave the sound of the pronunciation.

Nouns were simpler than verbs, we soon learned. There were 21 different kinds of verbs, each of which could be written 176 ways. When the affixes and suffixes were added, each could be written 800 different ways. To complicate the problems, some verbs lose letters or have their basic structure changed when run through the stem process. Add to this the active, passive, and reflexive changes and verbs are DIFFICULT.

He expected us to know the 21 kinds of verbs and to put even the most difficult words into the chart and write all 176 variations correctly. I remember our final exam after just one semester. This exam lasted 8 ½ hours and covered many pages. We had to know all about the language structure, to read and translate things we had never seen before, and recite the 23rd Psalm in Hebrew.

If we mispronounced one vowel in reciting the Psalm, he would not accept it. He would not tell us what vowel was wrong. We had to find our mistake and come back and say it right. After my third try I finally got it right. I can still recite this Psalm in Hebrew almost fifty years later.

I really struggled with this class and memorized things as I drove back and forth from Moweaqua to Lincoln. I sweat bullets trying to learn Hebrew, but I still use it weekly in my study and teaching.

They told me that for each hour in class they expected me to spend at least four hours out of class studying to prepare.

Preparing for my Advanced Introduction to New Testament class meant that I had to read a whole book almost every evening to complete the 4,750 pages of required reading. Thank the Lord that I had taken a class in speed-reading in college. At the end of the semester I was the only class member who had completed the reading over which we were tested. The other students had to request an extension to finish reading and to take the final exam.

As I drove to and from Lincoln I memorized Hebrew. This driving time helped me master some of the finer points of the language; I spent a lot of time in prayer over Hebrew.

Professor Ralls died while I was still at Lincoln. He was only 60 years old and had never had really good health in his whole life. He was writing the lexicon for one of the Semitic languages (Acadian) when he died. We had become very good friends. I still think of him with fondness.

Advanced Expository Preaching

Dr. Wayne Shaw had been a big part of recruiting me to Seminary. He was the Academic Dean of the Seminary and an exceptionally fine one. He also taught some classes. One of his classes was one of the most helpful of any I took while there. This class was called "Advanced Expository Preaching from the New Testament." He team taught this class with Bob Lowry, also a fine biblical scholar and preacher.

One of our assignments was to choose one New Testament book and make a complete bibliography of all the commentaries and preaching resources for it. I chose the book of Philippians.

After we had our bibliography finished, we were to make copies of it for each of the other students in the class. This meant that each student has a full biographical list for many New Testament books. We now had some very valuable resources for our New Testament preaching.

Dr. Shaw stressed that using topical and textual preaching, it takes 1,200 years to preach through the Bible. He said he expected each of us to commit to expositional preaching. And if we didn't, he would be very disappointed in us and our ministries would be deficient.

After this class I had enough material to preach to last five lifetimes; and I have mostly enjoyed this practice. On some occasions, preaching through Bible books has forced me to preach things I would have skipped over otherwise.

The Biblical Doctrine of Church

Harold Armstrong taught this class. He was one of the younger professors, and he and I often disagreed about his view of the church and we sort of debated in class. He broadened my view of the church and its importance to the world.

Abnormal Psychology

I was raised in a Christian home and in a very conservative part of America I was not prepared for what I learned about human behavior in this class. Even after taking the class, I felt sure humans did not do some of the things the class insisted they did. Unfortunately, I learned that people really did do these disgusting and degrading things the class said they did. It helped reinforce my belief in an actual Devil.

In this class we each had to write papers on some of our counseling sessions and these papers were critiqued in class with suggestions from the professor and class as to how we could do better. This improved our counseling skills considerably.

President of Intermountain Christian Convention

There were many other fine classes, too many to mention here without boring you. I asked Dr. Shaw to fill the pulpit for me very early in our ministry. I served on the Intermountain Church Planters organization while in Salt Lake City and was elected President just before leaving Utah. Each fall we had a three-day Christian Convention for the about 130 Christian churches in the Intermountain West.

This meant that I had to travel back to Montrose, Colorado for a Friday evening through Sunday convention. I gave the keynote address and led a workshop on Mormonism.

When my now good friend Bernard Carr learned we had to go, he and his wife, Pearl, wanted to go with us. He volunteered to drive his fine new Buick, which had returned to smelling normal. We left on Wednesday for the convention and left the convention Sunday afternoon in order for me to be back in class on Tuesday.

As I had already learned, Bernard was a speed demon. His new Buick had a device that could be set at the speed limit. If the limit was exceeded it would buzz. The speed limit was 70 mph. We drove many miles with the device buzzing as Bernard said he could not hear it.

The convention was well attended, but we received a panic phone call from Margaret's father, George, that her mother had brain cancer. It was one of the most vicious types and he pleaded for Margaret to come home to help him. Therefore Margaret flew to Seattle to be with her mother and father. Her mother was taken from Coos Bay, Oregon to Seattle, since that was where she could get the best care.

This meant that I traveled back to Moweaqua with the Carrs to care for our children, ministry, and seminary for the next three-and-one-half months without Margaret's help. After this time; Margaret's mother died at the age of 58 years. There were other complications back in Moweaqua that will be covered next.

When we announced the death of Margaret's mother at church, one of the members, John Gordon, came to me and asked, "Are you and the kids going to the funeral?" I told John, "I cannot afford to go as our schooling keeps us broke." He said, "I surmised as much, so Marge and I want to pay for you and your children to go home for the funeral. Here is a check all made out to you and signed; I have not put in the amount as you will need to do that." I looked at the check that was made out to me and the amount was blank. I said, "How much should I make it out for?" He said, "Could you use $25,000?" I gasped and said it was way too much. He then made out the check for $5,000 and gave it to me. It way more than covered our expenses.

The kids and I then drove to Coos Bay, Oregon, for the funeral. After the funeral we collected Margaret and traveled on to Los Angeles, California where I spoke at the North American Christian Convention before returning to Moweaqua and Seminary.

Teaching at the Seminary

While we were gone from Moweaqua for The Western Area Christian Convention and Margaret's mother's funeral, Dr. Wayne Shaw had filled the pulpit for me. He found a happy and growing church. The people were so loving and supportive of us and the building was full to overflowing. By that time many discouraged members had returned.

When we returned from Oregon and California, Dr. Shaw asked about our previous ministries in Oregon and Utah. He said there was one area of the Seminary curriculum that was deficient and the Board asked that he add a class on evangelism and church growth. He said the Board had agreed that I might be the person best qualified to teach such a class. I now had earned my Master of Arts degree, making me qualified to teach such a class at Seminary.

With much trepidation, I said I would pray about it and give him an answer in two weeks. This meant that I had to spend hours in the Seminary library searching books in print to find a suitable class textbook. After a lot of searching, I came up empty. I asked Dr. Strauss, the bibliography genius, about it. He had no suggestion for a good textbook for the class that were in the library or in print.

This made my teaching much more difficult than I anticipated. I prayerfully sat at my desk and made a chart of seventeen weeks, but I left each of the weeks blank. I then wrote in the subjects that should be covered. I took a small notebook for each week and began to brainstorm what each class should contain.

I soon became excited as the Lord had been preparing me for teaching this class for the past several years.

I taught the class for three semesters; the second semester of my second year in Seminary and both semesters the last full year. The first semester there were only about a dozen students. I questioned them and found that every one of them was preaching in one of the small churches in central Illinois. They all said they loved Seminary, but were discouraged by their church ministries. None reported baptisms or growth in their churches.

The class was a two-hour class on Tuesdays. We began class by my asking how many conversions they had, or if there were signs of growth. By the end of the first semester almost every week there were reports of baptisms and they were finding their ministries satisfying. Most of these small churches were in areas where there were many unsaved people.

The second semester of class there were 27 students and I was becoming a better teacher. One negative result was that some of the students were having such a good time in their ministries that they hated to take time to come to Seminary. To the best of my knowledge none dropped out of school.

One of the positive results for me was that I was doing the research for what would later become my doctoral dissertation. It was called, "A Practical Guide to Discipleship." It was published and became a college textbook for many years and was used on several continents.

Another benefit was that my teaching gave me free tuition. It did not cover Margaret's tuition, but my having free tuition really relieved our awfully tight budget. Without a doubt the person who learned the most was the young preacher/teacher.

Time for a New Parsonage

Just why there was a move to build a new parsonage is not really clear. It may have been that the various repair jobs that I did at the house had hit the village rumor mill. "Nothing much happens in Moweaqua but what you hear makes up for it."

Another reason may have been our popularity. Les Allison, one of the elders, was a fine builder who built quality homes throughout the county. He came and inspected the old manse and told me and the elders that it was beyond repair. The foundation had deteriorated and had major cracks in it. The roof was shot. The house was totally beyond repair. It would be throwing good money after bad to fix it. After 100-plus years of neglect it was beyond hope of fixing. It would be wiser to build a new one.

There was a water spring in the excavation for the old basement and due to the broken foundation, water constantly ran into the basement. This meant that a sump pump was necessary. This pump ran all the time if there was electricity. This worked fine until a thunder storm came up with torrential rains and the electricity went off. Then the basement filled with water because the electricity was off for several hours.

The water heater was up on concrete blocks so the pilot light would not flood out. Our washer and dryer were up on stacked concrete blocks. They were so high it was hard for Margaret to put clothes in the washer. The water would sometimes be 2–3 feet deep in the basement. When a storm came up the sump pump would short out when it was covered with water until the electricity came back on.

Repairing the heating and cooling would be an expensive endeavor. The old garage beside the house was rotting down. This old shack didn't look good next to the fine new church building. Some of the members were embarrassed that their preacher did not have better housing.

The church decided to tear down the old house and have Les Allison build a new one in the place of the old. Several farmers agreed to bring their farm machinery to help tear down the old house and excavate for the foundation of the new one. This proved to be no small task. The general consensus was that the old house had been built by farmers when they were not busy in the fields. It had been built like a fort.

The oak lumber had been nailed in place by old, square, handmade nails. When one nail would have sufficed, they had used four. I recall a huge tractor, attached by cable, to a big wood beam placed across inside the front wall of the house and trying to pull the wall down. The cable broke but the wall stood unmoved. Finally, with the aid of chain saws and more chains and cables, the wall was removed.

Of course we had to move out before the construction could begin. The only house in town available was a very small two bedroom house, still under construction, but not quite finished, since the owner ran out of money to finish it. The owner agreed we could rent it while the new parsonage was being constructed. There was no other place available. The church agreed to finish a couple of projects to make it livable, which in reality meant I would.

There were several problems. The wiring was not finished, nor was all of the plumbing. I agreed to finish up the wiring and plumbing. This turned into a massive job as bare electrical wires were exposed under the house. Fortunately I escaped being electrocuted. There were pools of water under the house from a recent torrential rain storm. The plumbing in the house was complete; but needed to be connected to the sewer line under the house. This took me hours.

Since we had furniture for a larger house and this one was dinky, we stored our things in one of the vacant church Sunday school classrooms. It was filled to the ceiling and to the door. We ended up with Margaret and me in one small bedroom and Carol Beth in the other and the boys sleeping in a small family room. We were cramped and had no washer, dryer, or dishwasher.

We had no more than moved in when Margaret's mother became ill. Margaret was gone for three-and-one-half months. I was now chief cook and launderer. I had to go to the local laundromat to wash clothes, which I often did in the middle of the night. Food was not gourmet, but with my humble efforts, we did not starve.

We lived there about six weeks when one evening a man came to the door. He said to me, "What are you doing living in my house? I have purchased this house and I am moving in tomorrow." I said, "You have to be kidding me!" He said, "No, and you have to get out today as my stuff will be coming tomorrow."

In a panic I called the prayer chain to begin to pray about our dilemma. In about an hour my phone rang and it was John Gordon. He said he had a solution for us. His father had died a few months before and his house was empty. We could move in. He said there was one problem; it was totally furnished and we would have to store the rest of our things. We solved the problem by using another class room and the Gordon mansion was a perfect solution. The beautiful old mansion was in reality a huge farm house with a barn and a shop.

We had seldom lived better. This was a well-maintained home with nice garage, shop, and barn next to it. The master bedroom bed even had a canopy over it. Each child had their own bedroom with all the furniture already there. The kitchen was very modern with a dishwasher. The laundry room had a modern washer and dryer.

The boys could play in the barn and work in the shop. There was a water trough for cattle to drink from, but no cattle. The boys caught fish in Flat Branch Creek, brought them home in buckets and put them in the tank. The boys helped with mowing the large lawn. When Margaret returned home, she had no idea where most of her things were, but we all loved the old Gordon mansion.

A crew of men and women descended on the small house late that afternoon and in about three hours we were set up in the mansion. (At the time of this move, Margaret was still with her dying mother in Seattle, Washington.)

Never could one hope to find finer people than there were in Moweaqua Christian Church. Of course we loved John and Marge Gordon, and this was the first of two times they rescued us in our hour of need. They would soon make it possible for us to go to Margaret's mother's funeral. God certainly does answer prayers and often uses His saints to do so.

After Margaret returned to Moweaqua, we all enjoyed this fine old home. One day we had a guest, Dan Acree, who had been a high school student when we were in Salt Lake City. He came to visit and he and I drove around the area seeing the sights and visiting.

When we returned to the house, it began to rain and so he and I sat in the car and visited in the garage that was not attached to the house. The rain increased until it was a torrential downpour. The town fire siren began to blow constantly. I said to Dan, "Why do they need the fire trucks, this rain would put out any fire?" It suddenly dawned on me that this was not a fire siren, but it was a tornado warning siren.

We jumped out of the car and I ran to the house to warn the family to head to the basement to guard against being killed by the storm. I ran back outside because I was worried about people living in the village across the street to the west. As our guest and I stood and looked, lo and behold, next to us were Margaret and the kids. She later said if I was to die she wanted to go along.

The rain stopped and was replaced by a terrible roaring like a speeding train coming towards us. In the distance, I saw this huge funnel cloud coming towards a row of the homes where members of the church lived, the Ringos, Allens, and several others.

People from these newer houses were rushing out and throwing themselves down in ditches filled with the torrential rain water. It was a fearsome sight. I prayed right out loud, "Lord Jesus, please protect everyone from this awful storm. Amen!"

As I said Amen, the tornado raised up over the houses and people, traveled a couple of hundred yards and then set down again, going out through the field leaving a wide swath through the crops that looked like it had just been plowed. The tornado was filled with rubbish like it was a giant vacuum cleaner.

I noticed that the storm, before it came to the row of houses, passed through our local cemetery. Later that day I went to see if there was any damage. One huge tombstone, about the size of a pickup truck bed, was missing. Some of the above ground tombs were gone along with those buried in what was a sort of above ground mausoleum. Some large pine trees were twisted off near the ground and totally gone. To the best of my knowledge none of the missing bodies, tombstones, or trees, were ever found.

I learned during our three plus years there that when the clouds turned dark to the west and then the sky sort of turned a strange green that a storm was coming. Usually these storms were only lightning and thunder, but sometimes they became tornadoes.

A few months later I was out one night visiting church members in their homes. It again was raining hard and the fire sirens began to blast. This time I was warned by the siren that there just may be another tornado coming. Suddenly all the lights went out in the whole town.

Here I was about half way to the house on the sidewalk, in a rain storm, in total darkness, when I heard the sound like a speeding railroad train coming directly towards me. What to do—stand still, run, throw myself on the ground, or just stand still and pray. I chose the latter and it sounded like the speeding railroad train passed just over the houses and me. I was so thankful that I was at peace with God since I was certain I was about to die.

I learned the next day that a tornado had passed over town a few hundred feet in the air. An old Indian legend told around town said that a tornado would never destroy Moweaqua. I learned that this legend was mostly just wishful thinking as I had come close to two tornadoes in just three years.

Speaking Engagements

A Southern Illinois Church

For the past three years I led workshops on Mormonism at the North American Christian Convention. Because of this I was often asked to speak at churches or conventions even while in Seminary. The first of these was at a church in Stewardson, Illinois. The date was September 16, 1973, not long after our arrival in Illinois.

This invitation came during my first semester in school. This Christian church in southeastern Illinois asked me to speak on a Sunday evening and they said they hoped to invite people from all over the county. When I arrived, the church building was packed with people wanting to learn about the Mormon religion.

The evening began with singing and then I began to speak. I indicated that I planned to offer a text-critical comparison of the Bible and Mormon scriptures. I would begin with the Bible, then the Book of Mormon, Doctrine and Covenants and the Pearl of Great Price. I would use a similar method to text-critically examine each of these books.

My discussion of the Bible went quite well, looking at it with what is called **MAPS**. I said that most Bibles have maps in the back of them. This is because the Bible is an actual record of real events. The Bible is supported by **M**anuscripts, **A**rchaeology, **P**rophecy and **S**tatistics. I gave supporting evidence for each category.

I next suggested that the Book of Mormon does not have maps in the back because it is not an actual history but an epic novel. As I proceeded, two rather pretty and sophisticated women stood up and began to yell at me. "You are a liar, hypocrite, servant of the Devil. You do not know what you are talking about." When the two of them had finally slowed down I said, "This is not your forum tonight, could I now proceed without your interruption?"

As I proceeded, they both stood up and again began to scream and shriek. If I said anything, they would scream so loud that I could not be heard. The ushers asked them to leave but they just screamed at them. Finally in desperation I collected my things from the pulpit and took a seat on the front row. The evening was over.

It just may have been the most effective way to demonstrate who is really behind the LDS religion. I left rather upset and ashamed, having no idea what the result of the evening would be. In my records I reported, "Two LDS ladies made a real fuss!"

The Iowa Christian Convention

Also in my first year in Seminary, I was invited to be the keynote speaker for the Iowa Christian Convention. One of the sessions was for me to speak about Mormonism. I again used the same information about comparing the Bible and Mormon scriptures that I used to teach LDS people and lead them to Christ. This study and speech eventually became the basis for a book, *The Bible and Mormon Scriptures Compared*, which would become my Master of Arts thesis. (When I turned in the thesis, all three faculty readers said this must be published. This book, ***The Bible and Mormon Scriptures Compared***, was first published in 1977 and is still in print and continues selling well.)

There was a huge crowd of about 2,500. So many wanted to learn about the Latter-day Saints church. The crowd listened intently. About half way through the lecture I paused and asked if there were any questions so far. A mature and dignified lady stood up and identified herself as a professor from the University of Iowa. She said she had a PHD and was a Mormon. An usher provided her with a microphone. She asked if she could address several questions to me about what I had been saying. She was polite, serious, and respectful. I gladly urged her to ask me any question she wished.

This became about a 20–25 minutes time of questions and answers, her questions and my answers. I had prayed earnestly before speaking that God would guide my mind and words. I wanted to glorify Him by every word spoken.

Never in my life have I ever found such liberty with information and scripture. I could quote long passages from the Bible with the exact chapter and verse references. These were passages that were familiar to me, but that I had never memorized. I also had a freedom to quote the Book of Mormon and Doctrine and Covenants. Again, these were passages that I was familiar with, but had never memorized. Each question was answered with the right words, but especially with the proper Bible texts and Mormon scriptures to support what had been said.

Our exchange was cordial and warm. It became clear to all that she had been given a lot of false information. When she came to the end of her questioning she said, "Why hasn't anyone told me these facts years ago: I have been wasting my life investing in a bunch of lies. I have been brainwashed."

I then finished my speech and thanked the Lord for sending her; the whole audience had watched as the information I had been giving was under close scrutiny. It just may have been the most powerful of any of the many lectures I have ever given on this subject.

For three-and-one-half years I was kept busy speaking at Midwestern churches. It added stress to an already too busy schedule.

Revival Meetings

While still in Salt Lake City, Utah, Roger Bankson and I had led a revival meeting in Smithfield, Missouri a couple of years before going to Seminary. The small church was led by Sid Allsbury, a nephew of George Allsbury, who had been my calling partner in Salt Lake City and who had died of cancer. Sid had asked me to come for a revival.

With Roger Bankson singing, the church was assured of capacity crowds. The small church would seat about 125 and the crowds were running well over 200. Chairs had to be used from all the classrooms. People were sitting in the nursery, on the stage and I barely had room to stand with people sitting on the stage right up to my feet. They had no baptistery so we had to go to the river evening after evening to baptize people. It was a wonderful time of spiritual enrichment and rejoicing. I was still in SLC for the first of the several Smithfield revival meetings in years to come.

I stayed with a wonderful older couple, Galen and Sylvia Fletcher, their home was in Kansas and the revival was in Missouri. The state line between Missouri and Kansas was the road in front of their house. They were gracious, southern Christians who made me feel loved like a member of their family.

Revival Meeting in Carthage

People from Carthage, Missouri, a nearby town, attended the second meeting in Smithfield and in November of 1973, Roger and I were invited to lead a revival at the Carthage Christian Church, which we did.

Hospitality was provided for Roger and me by the Dennis Crain family. They were not related to our family, but were fine Christian people who provided for our needs wonderfully.

Dennis had a wonderful event happen that week. He had put out a "drag line" across a local large creek. This was a fishing line stretched from bank to bank with hooks and shorter lines and hooks and bait fastened on the main line. He came in with a 45-pound cat fish. As you probably know a cat fish is ugly, but they are good to eat. We enjoyed some of his trophy fish for dinner.

The revival meeting was off to a good start with standing room only crowds even though this was a much larger church building. Roger's singing and solos were fantastic. I was preaching my heart out.

On Thursday evening the whole audience seemed under conviction. I could see and feel the response of the people building to the message and as I asked Roger to come lead the invitation hymn I expected many to come to Christ.

But the preacher jumped up and ran to the front of the auditorium, where he began to exhort the congregation. He called people out by name and told what their sins were and called them to repent. He spent twenty minutes haranguing the people and when he finished the revival meeting was over. It became clear the church's problem was not the people but the preacher. (Enough of this sad stuff as there were some other good things going on that week outside the revival.)

On Talk Radio

I was invited to speak on a local radio station in Joplin. It was a call-in talk show and I spoke on the Bible and Mormon Scriptures. For the first hour I talked and the second hour people called in and asked questions. The program lasted three days. The program was being listened to by people throughout the whole of southern Missouri and eastern Kansas. They advertised the program that was coming up to discuss Mormon Scripture and there appeared to be a large audience.

One man called and said his name was Jacob Hedrick, an Apostle of the Temple Lot Mormon Church. This group was called "The Hedrickites." He had all sorts of comments and questions. He asked if he could talk with me in person the next day. He attended the revival that evening.

We met and talked for a couple of hours each day for three days. Mainly our discussion was of Mormon Scripture. My experience had taught me that the real issue with the LDS is this: What is and is not scripture? If that issue is solved they really see how wonderful the Bible is and how awful their additional scriptures are. Then they are no longer LDS. We talked about the Bible, Book of Mormon, Doctrine and Covenants, and Pearl of Great Price.

It was clear to me that he was learning things that shook his faith in his church. The issues with the Book of Mormon, Doctrine and Covenants, and Pearl of Great Price are astounding. I could see the look of shock on his face because for the first time he really had a candid look at the multitude of problems with these supposed scriptures.

He came again the next day after I was finished on the radio. He had again listened to the program and was filled with questions. After our second and third meetings he expressed his thanks for all he had learned and that it was clear he had been misled by his church's teaching. His faith in the LDS movement was badly shaken. He was considered the Hedrickite Prophet and Apostle.

I learned to use the approach of looking at scripture rather than talking about such issues as Joseph Smith, polygamy, apostolic succession, baptism for the dead, or modern day prophets. If their scriptures are phony the whole system collapses.

A little background may be helpful. Joseph Smith started the Mormon religion in the 1830s, claiming to be a Prophet of God. He was shot and killed while quite young at the Carthage, Illinois jail, in a jail break. He had been given a revolver to protect himself because people were trying to break him and his brother Hyrum out of jail to possibly hang or kill them. He had shot all six shots of the revolver with one misfiring and with the other five shots it is reported that he brought men down. The church later reported that he died a martyr just like Jesus. Not quite true!

At his death, a succession plan to fill his place as leader was not firmly in place. Brigham Young took over the main church and installed himself as the next Prophet. This led to controversy since Joseph suggested his sons were to take over.

This led to having more than one LDS church soon after Joseph's death. Before long, there were seven major splits; and by the 1960s there were more than one hundred minor splits. (This number was reported to me by the Daughters of the Utah Pioneers Museum in Salt Lake City.)

The man I was studying with was an Apostle in one of these seven groups, "The Hedrickites," or "Temple Lot" as they were called. He was their chief leader or Prophet. This church was small with, not twelve, but only three Apostles.

This group was important since they had control of "Temple Lot." This was the piece of property where Joseph Smith prophesied a temple would be built. It would happen in his lifetime, before the original group of apostles had all died. (This prophecy and none of any of Smith's about fifty other prophecies have ever came true as he predicted.) No temple has been built there yet, but the property was owned by the Temple Lot group and this small group was where a part of Joseph Smith's family members were attending.

Jacob told me, at that time, there were just three Apostles in the Temple Lot LDS church. After our third study, I did not have further contact with him. I was so busy with ministering to the Moweaqua church and attending Seminary that I gave little further thought to him or this group for several years.

Five years later after I had graduated from Seminary and we were now living in Caldwell, Idaho, where I was the preacher of First Christian Church. I was home one Monday morning when the doorbell rang. When I answered the door, I thought I knew the man.

My first words were, "I know you, where have we met before?" He said he had never seen me before and we had not met. When he said his name, it dawned on me that he looked very much like his great-great-great grandfather, Joseph Smith. I had seen many pictures of his grandpa, and he looked remarkably like him.

He introduced himself and said again that his name was Joseph Smith and that he was an Apostle in the Temple Lot LDS church. Bells immediately began to ring in my head as I recalled meeting with Jacob Hedrick years before. I invited Joseph into our home so we could visit.

Joseph said he had been given a book I had written and he had questions about it that he wanted to ask me. The book was *The Bible and Mormon Scriptures Compared.* This book was a best seller in bookstores across America. Joseph Smith was living in Horseshoe Bend, a small Idaho town near Boise.

As we visited we looked at the multitude of proof there is for the accuracy and inspiration of our Bible and proof of who Jesus was and is. This we agreed upon—the Bible is the inspired word of God and Jesus is the Savior.

When we began to look at the Book of Mormon, Joseph became quite agitated. When I showed him that there were more than 4,000 mistakes in the original Book of Mormon he was incredulous. Joseph Smith had said the Book of Mormon was the most correct book on earth. These 4,000 mistakes in the original Book of Mormon average seven mistakes on each side of each page.

When I showed him some of the untrue stories in the Book of Mormon, like 2 Nephi the fifth chapter, he really was disturbed. We proceeded no further that day and he agreed to come back the following Monday at the same time.

On our second meeting I pointed out that Section One in the Doctrine and Covenants said that these prophecies were from God and would never pass away. I had brought, from my office, an original copy of the Doctrine and Covenants. On page seven it said these were God's words and would never pass away or change, but on page eleven half of a page had been taken out. I showed him that there were 27 doctrinal reversals from the original edition to the present one. God's unchanging word was repeatedly changed. This information is shocking to any LDS person when first confronted with it. We then looked at the Pearl of

Great Price, another of their supposed scriptures, with its glaring faults.

He asked to return again the third Monday morning, which he did. This time he brought a rather large book with him. He explained that three of the early LDS divisions all wanted the Temple Lot in Independence, Missouri, since Joseph Smith had prophesied that in his lifetime, and the present LDS Apostles lifetime, a Temple would be built there.

There had been multiple lawsuits between the three groups, the LDS Utah Branch, the Reorganized Church of Jesus Christ and The Hedrickites. This book contained photocopies of the hundreds of pages of transcripts from the several lawsuits between these groups trying to get the property from the Hedrickites. He offered to let me keep the book for a few weeks until I had time to read and study it.

I was flabbergasted when I got into it. This was where the dirty laundry of this modern-day cult had been examined in public. They sort of "spilled the beans" on each other.

After three more weeks Joseph wanted his book back, but he agreed that I could keep a photo copy for my library, which I have. Much of this book is boring, but there are many insights for the history of Mormonism buff.

The revival back in Carthage, Missouri was a failure, but the radio program was helpful to thousands. The meetings with the two Temple Lot Church Apostles may have been helpful, but the outcome has remained unknown to me. Hopefully they were pointed to the real Jesus and away from Joseph Smith the false Prophet.

Back at Seminary

Guest Lecturers

Lincoln Christian Seminary had top quality professors; but it was also a policy to occasionally bring in outside lecturers who were specialists in their respective fields of study and teaching.

These sessions would sometimes be for as long as two or more weeks and last all or most of the day until a full semester of work was completed. One of my favorite lecturers was Dr. Roland Bainton, who was at the Seminary for three weeks. This was in October of 1974.

Dr. Bainton was for many years, the Titus Street Professor of Church History at Yale University and one of America's foremost church historians. Dr. Bainton, now deceased, was esteemed by scholars and laymen alike for his perceptive writing in the field of Christian history. His writings offered penetrating insights, rare dramatic artistry in writing, and added depth since he was also an ordained minister. He has written a wide array of books on the history of the church in which his combined talents as minister, theologian, master teacher, and author have produced Christian literature of unusual quality.

Dr. Bainton was born in Ilkeston, Derbyshire, England, and came to America when he was eight years old. He earned his doctorate from Yale University. His lectures were marvelous; I purchased three of his books that have become some of my favorites about the Sixteenth Century Reformation.

The three books are:

The Reformation of the Sixteenth Century
Erasmus of Christendom
Here I Stand, a Life of Martin Luther

Dr. Bainton's books, in my opinion, are as fine as any ever written on the subjects he covers. His lectures stressed the desire of the reformers to return to biblical teaching and standards. After Dr. Bainton's lectures, one felt like they knew the reformers personally. When I read his book on Martin Luther, his account was so clear and real, that when Luther died I cried.

Unfortunately, according to Dr. Bainton, after the deaths of the reformers, some of their followers wanted to memorialize them. They did not follow through on some of their teachings. For example, Luther had clearly said that people should call themselves Christians, not Lutherans.

Most of the reformers had been Catholics and were reacting against the many doctrinal departures of the Catholic Church from scriptures. Luther had posted his 95 Theses on the door of the Wittenberg, Germany, church door.

He listed his ninety-five objections to Catholic doctrine and practices and he concluded by saying:

> "Out of love for the truth and from a desire to elucidate it, the Reverend Father Martin Luther, Master of Arts and Sacred Theology, and ordinary lecturer therein at Wittenberg, intends to defend the following statements and to dispute on them in that place. Therefore, he asks that those who cannot be present and dispute with him orally shall do so in their absence by letter. In the name of our Lord Jesus Christ, Amen."

One conclusion, from Dr. Bainton's lectures, was that the reformers saw the Bible as the authority for church doctrine. Luther, Erasmus, Conrad Grable, Calvin, the translators of the New Testament, Wittenberg and Wycliff, and most of the reformers, were reacting against the errors and doctrinal fallacies of the corrupt church.

These men were interested in and had studied the original biblical languages of Hebrew and Greek. Luther translated the New Testament from Greek into German. It was called, "The September Testament." It was reported that he did this all in sixteen weeks. This is still primarily the New Testament used by the German people today.

Sometimes their reactions against Catholic doctrine went too far. This is called "The Swinging of the Pendulum." This means going from one extreme to the opposite extreme. For example, in Calvin's reaction to the Catholic doctrine of salvation through works, he went to the opposite extreme of salvation by grace alone. It is true that salvation is by grace, but not grace alone.

What a wonderful blessing it was to be able to hear some of the finest theologians of our time at the Seminary. Among those who came, Dr. Bainton stands out most clearly as my favorite visiting professor.

Problems Connected to Building the New Parsonage

Elder Les Allison was not only a godly elder, but a first-rate builder. When the old manse was torn down, there remained a large hole in the ground that soon filled about half full of water. This required that a sump pump be installed lower than the foundation hole that would contain the basement of the new house. When this was installed and the hole dried out, the new floor and foundation were installed.

The new sump pump that was installed had a battery backup for the times when the electricity was off due to thunder storms or other reasons.

Wayne and Evelyn

One family in the church was Wayne and Evelyn Wooters. They owned the largest farm in the county. Wayne farmed this gigantic ranch and was not too shy in letting people know he was affluent. Evelyn was noted for her ability to correct people with whom she disagreed. There was no filter between her brain and tongue.

After a couple of episodes with Evelyn, I was informed that her mother and father had both been deaf mutes. She was never taught at home to hold her tongue. Since her parents could not hear, they had no idea what she was saying. Unfortunately, the rest of the community could still hear her.

Years later I was visiting with the two ministers that had followed me in Moweaqua. We were talking at the North American

Christian Convention. The one who was still the preacher said to us two past preachers, "I wish I was as godly as you two brothers." We asked why he would say such a thing to us. He replied, "Well, you two got along with everyone, but there is this woman in the church that just tries my patience to the breaking point." We responded in unison, "Evelyn!" We all laughed and then told of some of the more notable events with Evelyn. We each had gruesome stories to relate.

Unfortunately for Wayne was the fact that Evelyn was beautiful and he had not discovered her tongue problem until after they were married. Over the years this had led to him also being rather difficult to talk with. He had sort of picked up her contrary spirit, maybe in self-defense. This was one of the reasons why he was never chosen as an elder.

When Les Allison had the house finished, he took me to the basement and showed me that it had been plumbed for a water softener. He took me to the old church building and showed me a perfectly good water softener that had been hooked up to the old baptistery which was no longer used. Les suggested that I move it to the new house so the awful city water would not ruin all the new plumbing, and the washing machine.

A couple of weeks later I found time to disconnect it from the baptistery that was no longer used and hooked it up in the parsonage. It worked fine and I felt good to have been a part of the new project.

Wayne Wooters had been made chairman of the Building and Grounds committee. He came into my office and asked to talk with me. He sat down and said, "Someone stole the water softener from the old church building baptistery. I thought about filing a complaint with the police department but decided if the crook could be found maybe he might just replace it and I would not have to get the police involved. Could you help me solve this problem without any further issue?" It was clear to me that he knew that I moved it. Not wanting to cause problems, I did not tell him an elder and the builder, Les Allison told me to do it.

I asked Les Allison what to do. He said that he did not want a confrontation with Wayne and Evelyn so I should just return it. So a few days later I disconnected it and while hauling the heavy tank up the basement stairs, it slipped out of my hands and tumbling down the stairs it broke as it hit the cement floor at the foot of the stairs.

Somehow Wayne learned that I was trying to replace it and called to say, "The water softener must be replaced by a licensed plumber, not some amateur." So now I had to purchase a new one and pay for it to be installed by a plumber. This cost me hundreds of dollars that I did not have, thank goodness for a credit card. When I saw this new water softener in the old building sitting unused, it always was a sore point to me. At the same time we paid to have one installed in the new parsonage.

But, that is not the end of the story. Evelyn was made chairperson by her husband for the new parsonage decoration committee. It took weeks for her committee to decide what color of paint, carpet and floor coverings were to be used. Her words were, "I am trying to find colors that will fit with the next preacher's things." Finally the interior was painted and the floor coverings were installed so we could move in after experiencing weeks of delay.

Then it was time for Evelyn's committee to pick window coverings. She kept saying, "We need to really save money on drapes. I don't want to pay more for them than the poorest people in the church can afford."

We had an elder and his wife from Salt Lake City visiting us. Ruth happened to be in the room when Evelyn's committee met. When Ruth heard Evelyn talk about cheap drapes Ruth spoke up and said, "I would think Christians would want their preacher to have nice drapes, not cheap junk." Evelyn got up angrily and stormed out of the house crying.

For six months we lived in the new house without window coverings. This was especially problematic in our bedroom. There were three big windows that looked out towards the church building and church parking lot. This parking lot had bright lights that burned all night.

The church shared the back parking lot with M&W grocery store that was next door to the church building. The store was open late during the week and people in the parking lot or church building could look right into our bedroom windows.

For six months we crawled from our bed to the toilet during the night. Dressing was also a problem; we had to take our clothes into the bathroom to dress and undress. Needless to say I promised Margaret that never again would we live in a church parsonage.

The Wooters were allowed to behave like this since they used their money as a weapon to control others' behavior. Yes, all three preachers agreed Evelyn was the only real problem in this wonderful church full of great Christians. We laugh when we think of us crawling around the bedroom floor as adults.

Another Story Worth Telling

After completing Seminary, one event in our next ministry needs to be included in this narrative. It had to do with Discipleship. As already mentioned, I taught the last two years of attendance at Lincoln Christian Seminary. The class I taught was about Christian Discipleship. The idea was founded on putting every Christian to work. The class offered ways to implement Jesus' command to "Go into all the world and make disciples..." (Matthew 28:18).

When arriving in Caldwell, Idaho, as their new preacher, these ideas were fresh in my mind. Almost immediately we began a group called "Bold Ones for Christ." The idea was taken from Ephesians 6:19 where Paul mentions that he wants to open his mouth boldly to proclaim Christ.

We announced that we would welcome 12 individuals into the group called "Bold Ones for Christ." This would be a commitment for nine months and would require each person to commit Tuesday evening most weeks for the nine months. We would meet for a provided meal and teaching, and then we would go out to proclaim Christ. This group grew and we repeated it each year with additional old and new members. The group grew to about 24 regulars.

Several from this group went on to enroll in Bible college and ended up as preaching ministers. Such men as Larry Bucy and Clayne Beck are examples. One of the members was Al Harshman, a very wealthy farm owner and real estate investor.

Al and I became warm friends; he attended class and we called together for a couple of years. The following events happened years later, after I had become President of Boise Bible College.

Al became ill and it was so serious that he was taken to the Mayo Clinic in Scottsdale, Arizona. His wife, Jackie, called to tell me that the doctors were predicting that Al would soon die, possibly within two weeks.

When I heard this, I flew to Phoenix, rented a car and went to visit my dear brother. There were three of us in the room that first evening—myself, Jackie, and a Christian friend of Jackie's, Deborah Eddie, who was Al's home doctor's wife. After talking with Al, it was suggested that we lay hands on Al and pray over him.

We did, and as I recall my prayer went something like this, "Dear Lord Jesus, please hear our united prayer of faith for your son Aldon Harshman; will you send a Holy Angel to minister to him tonight, that he might be healed and in two weeks be able to go home and live well for at least a year to finish his business and organize his life and affairs. We will thank and praise you for hearing and answering this prayer of faith. Amen, thank you Jesus." We left Al and we drove to our lodging together in my rented car.

Remember, Al was critically ill, with a colostomy, internal infections, possibly eaten up inside with cancer, and dying. When we returned in the morning and came into his hospital room all Al could do was sob. When he tried to talk he was overcome with tears and sobbing.

Finally, he gained enough control of himself to tell us this story. Al said, "I was sitting up in bed about midnight in terrible pain when a man dressed in white stood at the foot of my bed; I was totally awake and not dreaming. This man said to me 'I am the Angel Gabriel and the Lord Jesus Christ has sent me to give you this message. You are going to recover and go home well in two weeks and He has granted you a year to finalize your affairs before you are called home.'" Al insisted to the three of us that this really happened and that it was not a dream.

What confirmed in my mind that this really did happen was that in two weeks Al was remarkably recovered, sent back home and did live many months before he was called home. During that time he and I continued to fellowship and go out to lunch.

One day he let me drive his beautiful Bentley car as we went to lunch. It was dirty and he wanted me to take it through the car wash I used. As I pulled in, the manager asked that I roll down the window and asked me what my new car was. "Is it a Chrysler product? Bet it cost you at least $70,000." Al leaned over and said to him, "Son, try again, it is a Bentley, one of a kind, and it cost me $500,000."

Here again was this hospital event that had all the markings of miraculous. Was it Gabriel? Was Al dying? Did he miraculously recover? Did he go home in two weeks? Did he live another whole year? It appears that the answer to each of these questions is almost certainly yes! Yes, Holy Angels are sent out to do service to Christians and it appears that the Lord did all of this for his diligent, humble, and generous son Aldon Harshman (Hebrews 1:14).

During that year Al gave Boise Bible College a personal check for one million dollars and might have given more if his life had been extended longer. He is lovingly remembered as a godly friend. I hope to spend time with him in Heaven.

Preaching and Teaching

When Sundays came, I was loaded with wonderful things to preach and teach that I was learning at Seminary. I began an adult class during the Sunday school hour in the old church building's chapel. This soon filled up with people. I had taught Bible Survey for years but now had lots of great additional material to present.

On Wednesday evenings I also taught an adult class and covered some of the great new things that I was learning at Seminary. The church expressed surprise that their previous preachers had not availed themselves of the chance to study at Lincoln Christian Seminary since it proved such a blessing to the whole church.

I returned to Moweaqua to preach after being gone for about five years. The elder that introduced me said, "Charles introduced our church to biblical scholarship." Being their preacher introduced me to what a really mature Christian church looked and felt like. Our time there was very happy, except for Evelyn. I pray she is not on a decoration committee in Heaven, and hope she made it there.

Our years in Moweaqua were happy and wonderfully blessed years. So many people grew in their faith. Nearly one hundred gave their lives to Jesus, were baptized and grew strong in their faith.

The relationship with the mortician in the church led to me having many funerals for people from the Job's Daughter's Home near Moweaqua. Very early I was asked to have a funeral. Even though these funerals were attended often by just the funeral director and a couple of people from the home, I gave a regular funeral message and prayers.

The mortician said this was unusual. Other preachers read a verse, prayed and asked for the honorarium. He asked why I did much more. My reason was that almost always there were at least one or more unsaved people present. This was my chance to witness to them. Before long, I was asked to have almost all of these funerals. Sometimes the honorarium was as much as $100, which was a big help to our limited budget.

Monday Night Football and a Few Beers

The statement that went around Moweaqua was not always true, "Nothing ever happens in Moweaqua, but what you hear makes up for it." Let me explain:

Carol Beth made a friend of Kevin from the Conservative Baptist Church in town. Kevin came to our house to visit her and noticed the chess set that was on the table in the living room of the new parsonage. He informed me that he was a champion chess player and asked if I knew how to play. I said yes. He challenged me to a game and I agreed.

The first game I beat him in three moves. This was the case for all of the three games we played that evening. I then explained to Kevin that I had belonged to the chess club in high school and had played a lot of chess.

Well, Kevin somehow got me acquainted with their preacher at their church. When I met the preacher he asked me what I thought about church leaders drinking beer. This led to the following discussion.

His question centered in Paul's instruction to Timothy, "No longer drink only water, but use a little wine for the sake of your stomach and your frequent ailments" (I Timothy 5:23 ESV).

I asked the preacher if the Bible contradicts itself. He replied that he was sure it didn't. I suggested that we look at Proverbs 23:29–35, where Solomon forbids drinking fermented alcoholic wine. We read the passage. He then said, "Why does Paul then tell Timothy to do so?"

He explained that one of their church leaders was insisting that it was just fine for him to watch Monday night football and drink a few beers. The man's wife complained that her husband became hard to get along with after a few beers. She had come to hate Monday night football.

Here is what I showed the fellow preacher. In the New Testament there are two Greek words for wine, "Oinos" and "Gleukos." Both are translated "wine" in our New Testament and neither, inherent in the word, indicate whether it is alcoholic wine or grape juice. Neither word necessarily means alcoholic drink like we use the word wine today.

For example, take the word "wine-press," or "new wine skins." When grapes are pressed, does one get alcoholic juice? No, we get grape juice. Both of the Greek words that are translated wine can be used for grape juice or alcoholic drink in the New Testament. We have to consider the context to learn whether it was fermented or not. They did not have fortified liquor like we have today. It took hours of drinking alcoholic wine to get really drunk.

Would Paul have told the church that an elder was not to drink wine, meaning grape juice? Would Paul tell deacons they should not drink much wine, or grape juice? The answer to this question is that the Bible warns against drinking alcoholic beverage, not grape juice. An elder is not to drink any alcoholic wine, while maybe a deacon might drink a very little.

Now back to the church leader at the other church. This was a very small church. Kevin said to me that this man kept a good supply of cold beer in his refrigerator. It became a matter of discussion around their church.

Macon Street ran in front of our house and north and south. At the south end of the street, at the edge of town, was a sharp 90-degree corner and the street then ran East out into the farm land and on to Lake Shelbyville, about twenty miles away.

The son of the beer-drinking church leader brought two high school girls home from school with him one afternoon. Both parents were gone so he suggested that the three of them have a few cold beers. They each imbibed. His judgment was now somewhat impaired so he suggested that they take his mom's new Ford car for a drive. He had been taking driver's education and felt qualified to drive it. The two girls agreed and off they went out into the countryside towards Lake Shelbyville.

On their way back home, with the warm day and time, the beer had taken full effect on the boy and he tried to take the 90-degree curve, at the end of our street, at an estimated 90 miles an hour. The car rolled, throwing all three out, since none wore seat belts.

The boy and one girl were killed instantly and the other girl survived, but was left a paraplegic for the rest of her life. Of course the whole town grieved.

Sometimes tragic things did happen in Moweaqua. Over the years many tragic events have transpired in my ministry that had their beginning with "just a few beers at Monday night football," or some other place or event. I can think of no blessing having ever come out of just having a few beers. Alcohol changes a person's personality, removes moral restraint, and destroys judgment. Today one person in nine who drinks socially will become an alcoholic. Solomon, in Proverbs, was right, don't drink alcoholic beverages. A better choice might be a cup of coffee, glass of iced tea, a soda, or milk.

A Young Preacher Goes to Seminary

What About the Preaching Ministry?

The preceding history in this book is from about three-and-one-half years of the young preacher's life. Would it be fair to say these had been productive and exciting? Much of what was accomplished was not due to his skill or giftedness, but that the Lord Jesus had multiplied and amplified his humble efforts.

The added benefit of the extended education had provided quality and depth to what was already a blessed ministry. Education placed so many valuable tools to the ministry to make the preacher even more used of God.

Looking back at these years, now from old age, it is so clear that God had often placed him in places where someone, though not especially talented, would represent His truth and the Holy Scriptures would, to the best of his limited ability, speak to the needs of the people. God will use you to His glory if you will seek to follow His leading.

There are few if any other professions where a person's life can count to such wide benefit for humanity. There are very few jobs that will provide such varied and glorious experiences, while at the same time turning hundreds, if not thousands to life in Christ and eternal salvation.

Now looking back at everyone from high school, at members of the extended family and people from hundreds of worthy occupations, where could a person better invest their life than in preaching the Gospel of the grace and mercy of Jesus Christ.

This book is written with the goal of pointing the finest of our young men and women to ministry for Christ and His church. The nation must have a new wave of preachers, evangelists, Christian musicians, and youth leaders to turn America away from the brink of destruction, socialism, and ruin. We must extend the call for a new wave of religious leaders to bring revival to our failing nation.

When we issue this call to ministry to the best of our next generation, we will be pointing them to professions of glorious productivity and rewards in their lives that are beyond imagination.

Core Values

A revival meeting was going on at our church back home when I was a kid of thirteen years. The evangelist was Archie Word and our preacher was Stuart Baker. Both were men of integrity.

Earlier in my life I had been baptized, but I knew it was a farce from the day it was done. It was a hot summer day and our church building had no air conditioning. I was sitting between two of my buddies, the Ledford brothers, Edwin and Roy. Edwin leaned over and whispered to me, "It sure is hot in here, bet the water in the baptistery would sure feel good. Might be almost like going swimming." We three agreed to give it a shot so responded to the invitation and were baptized.

From the start I knew it was a hypocritical act and I was secretly ashamed. I was often under conviction about what I had done and knew I had to make it right, but everyone thought that little Chuckie was a Christian and I was embarrassed to admit that I wasn't.

We were having a revival meeting; Brother Word's powerful preaching cut to my heart and on December 13, 1951, I was the first to respond to the invitation to commit my life to Christ. As I recall, many others came also, including my older brother David.

It was probably the coldest day of my youth and our church didn't have central heat. We had to wait for the baptistery to be filled, otherwise it would have frozen during the cold days and nights. When we got in the water, Brother Baker had on fishing boots with wool socks and a wool suit, but I was in my Levis. He testified and prayed and I grew more and more chilled. It was nothing like my first baptism when it was so hot. Maybe this was God's way of rewarding my previous hypocrisy.

After we exited the baptistery, before I could even dress, the preacher said to me, "Raise your right hand and promise God these five things." I was shaking and am not sure if it was the Holy Spirit or just the cold water, possibly both. This I promised and have done so. I have thanked Stuart Baker and God ever since. These five things have been the core values of my Christian life. Here they are:

1. Always go to church.
2. Never miss communion.
3. Pray at least five times each day.
4. Regularly study your Bible.
5. Tithe your money and time.

These have been the core values of my Christian life and are why God has been so faithful in blessing our humble ministry and the work in His church. Even though I was so very busy while in Seminary, these habits had been so ingrained that they were a regular part of my daily life.

Today I love the church more than life. In the 68 years, since I was baptized, I have not missed communion even one Sunday. Sometimes it was at 35,000 feet and at 540 miles an hour in a jet airplane, traveling to some distant land to preach and teach. But, without fail, we have observed the Lord's Supper always; what a huge blessing. When wonderful things happened, Jesus met us there to rejoice with us. When tragedy stuck, Jesus has always met us there to comfort and strengthen us.

Praying as I get out of bed in the morning and at meal times and again upon going to bed has been expanded into times of prayer all through the days and nights.

I have worn out many Bibles and taught it through about 50 times. It has become a part of who I am and how I think and act. One is not well educated until they know the Holy Bible.

These are the Core Values that need to be a part of every Christian's life. If they are a part of your life you will never backslide or fall away. A preacher must have these traits of faithfulness. Oh How I Love Jesus!

Tithing has been one of the finest financial blessings in our family. God has so often repaid our small and regular gifts with many huge and wonderful gifts. One Christian brother gave us a gift of $100,000. It just showed up in my checking account. I asked him why and he said, "Oh, God has been blessing me and laid it on my heart to share it with you." Sometimes in the hour of our greatest need the Lord has given us unbelievable support and love.

We did not keep this gift but returned it to George Hafer with the request that when I saw a great need could I come ask for his help. George agreed, and he and his wife, Jane, sent about a dozen young men to Seminary, paying their expenses. These men continue to serve Christ across the world today.

At the basis of the life of the preacher and Christian are these five simple values. Want to be blessed? Give your life to Jesus. Want to remain faithful? Make these five things priorities in your life. Want to use your life to the fullest? If qualified, be a preacher of the gospel. There is no more important or fulfilling work than preaching the gospel. Amen.

Epilogue

After three-and-one-half years in Seminary I had earned the Master of Arts degree in Christian Education and the Master of Divinity degree in Ministry. These were wonderful years, but grueling. I had gone to school full time and also ministered to a great church. Both degrees were earned with honors.

These two degrees were conferred at two different ceremonies two years apart. The ceremonies were glorious and held in the great Phillips Memorial Chapel. (A picture of this chapel is on the front of this book.) As the degrees were granted, the proper gorgeous masters collars were placed around our necks. The colors reflected what degree had been earned.

To fulfill the requirements of the Master of Arts degree, I was required to write a thesis. My degree was in Christian Education so I chose the subject of teaching Mormons and leading them to salvation in Jesus Christ. The thesis ended up being called, "The Bible and Mormon Scriptures Compared." The sub-title was "The Educational Process of Leading a Mormon to Christ."

When the thesis was submitted to the evaluation committee of three professors, Doctors Shaw, Wilson, and Mills, all three said it needed to be published.

My desire had been to continue on and earn a doctorate in Ministry. My research was directed to two schools, Duke Divinity School and Luther-Rice Seminary in Jacksonville, Florida. I ended up choosing Luther-Rice for several reasons.

After considerable research, I was accepted into both programs but Duke had a three-year wait before I could enroll. In addition, Luther-Rice's degree programs better fitted my educational goals.

Luther-Rice advertised their program as the most comprehensive and difficult doctoral program in America. They had pioneered the Doctor of Ministry degree program many years before and now nearly fifty seminaries offered programs patterned similar to theirs.

This degree required a lot of work before one could even enroll. They wanted a transcript of my education from the first grade through the Master of Divinity. They wanted to have a list of all of the textbooks I had used from college and seminary.

They required that I send them a list of all the books in my library. They wanted a written history of my conversion and call to ministry. Later I understood why they had asked for all of this information.

When finally fully accepted into the program, I was to choose four majors from a list of seventy-five possibilities. They then explained that one of the things I would learn was how to design a doctoral program as I would next have to help design and choose all of the textbooks for each major. After I had fleshed out the four majors, I would submit the program for evaluation and possible acceptance.

The four majors I had chosen were:

1. Communication
2. Administration
3. Spiritual Development
4. Writing.

I learned that each major had six units of study and each unit had their own text or texts. I was to choose these texts and they all had to be something I had never studied or read before. My major professor offered assistance in helping me make these choices, often refusing the volume I had chosen, suggesting there were better options.

This meant that for Communication I had at least six textbooks. In unit one in Communication I was to submit three sermons. The first Topical, second Textual, and third was to be Expository. In preaching I was to repeat this process three times, or submit nine sermons. Three were evaluated and returned to me for correction before I submitted the next three.

In preparation, I was to translate the scripture text from the original language. I was to submit my translation notes. I then was to consult at least three commentaries and submit my study notes. I was to brainstorm the sermon and submit my notes, then write the sermon out and preach it, but record it and submit a printed copy of the recording and corrected as to how I should have preached it.

This was just one of the six requirements for Communication. Another Communications units of study was teaching, which required me to cover the book of Hebrews with writing the lessons, teaching, transcribing, submitting, correcting, and resubmitting.

In addition, in Communication, I was to cover the rites of the church: funerals, weddings, baptisms, and communion. Fortunately, I had a full-time secretary who helped me almost full time for a year in making lists, and transcribing my recorded sermons and lessons.

This was only the first of four majors. Similar exhaustive work was required in each of the four majors. In Administration I had to study the past twenty-five years of the church. I had to report attendance, giving and teaching. I was to write a comprehensive review of everything about the church from whom the preachers were, elders, classes, sermon topics, baptisms, income, budget, new members, etc.

After a careful study of the past I was to cover every department of the church for twenty-five years into the future with plans for everything that should be done, with staff, funding, evangelism, building, etc.

I was to write job descriptions and lay out the plans for the future of the church in every department: worship, buildings, evangelism, education, missions, and whatever I deemed wise.

All of these plans had to be developed and submitted a third, another third and the final third. All of this was to be examined by my major professor with his recommendations as to how to improve my plans for the second and third presentations.

Similar things were expected in all four majors. At the end of this 18-month period I had written a stack of papers almost two feet high. Also I had to write my doctoral dissertation that had to be submitted three times as it progressed, to be critiqued, corrected by me, rewritten by me, and returned.

This dissertation was entitled, "A Practical Guide for Discipleship" or how to build an evangelistic church. This book was finally accepted and they suggested publication. It was published and has been used as a college textbook for many years.

Luther-Rice Seminary had a large enrollment during the period I was there and associated with the seminary and college. There were more than 500 people in the doctoral program and many became well known for their achievements in ministry. Spiro Zodhiates became one of the leading experts in Koina Greek in the United States. Another man, Stephen Olford, became known as the prince of Baptist preachers. Another became a member of the U.S. President's cabinet. The preacher of the largest Assembly of God church in America attended at the same time. John Whitcomb Jr., son of the famous author, was there and went on to become a Christian college professor and president. It was a time of great intellectual growth and the things learned are still a blessing almost every day.

Finally the work was completed, tuition payed, dissertation accepted and it was time to graduate. Graduation was held at the Great Southern Baptist Church in Jacksonville, Florida.

On the day of the graduation service from the college and seminary, this gigantic building was packed to the balconies. There were nearly five hundred doctoral graduates alone. The building was beautiful and behind the stage was a large baptistery with a stream running down the front of the building into the baptismal pool.

Music was glorious, speeches were extraordinary, and finally the President of the University, Dr. Robert Witty, arose to speak. He welcomed us one by one and as we received our degrees each of us received our doctoral degrees and the collar that told what our earned degree was in. It was a great and impressive ceremony, never to be forgotten.

My mother and step-father, Jessie and Singleton Edwards, and beloved Aunt Delores Hammett were present, having come all the way from Oregon.

This was the culmination of eleven-and-a-half years of full time attendance of college and seminary. My doctor, Charles Krause, M.D., said to me, "Charles, it is time for you to quit going to school and work the rest of your life." I took his advice.

Other Books by Dr. Charles A. Crane

1. *Do You Know What the Mormon Church Teaches?*
   (A brief comparison of Bible teaching and Mormon Doctrine)

2. *Mormon Missionaries in Flight*
   (Why a Mormon Missionary does not want to talk to a knowledgeable Christian)

3. *The Bible and Mormon Scriptures Compared*
   (A Text Critical comparison of the Bible and Mormon Scriptures)

4. *Ashamed of Joseph*
   (An accurate biography of Joseph Smith)

5. *Christianity and Mormonism, from Bondage to Freedom*
   (Christ brings freedom from Mormon bondage)

6. *Is Mormonism Christian?*
   (This is a rewrite of Harry Ropp's fine book after his untimely death.)

7. *Autobiography of Charles A. Crane*

8. *A Practical Guide to Soul Winning* (Discipleship)
   (Biblical management of the church for evangelism and growth)

9. *Personal Family Finance*
   (Becoming affluent with modest income)

10. *The Bible—The True and Reliable Word of God*
    (The result of fifty years of study of ancient Biblical manuscripts)

11. *The Families of Man Archaeologically and Biblically Traced* (Humanity today can be traced back to Noah and the Ark)

12. *The Adventures of a Young Preacher* (A fun book showing the value of preachers)

13. *Irrefutable Proof that Jesus Is the Messiah.* (Three things that are positive proof we have a Savior)

14. *Adventures of a Young Preacher in Salt Lake City* (Volume 2 in the Young Preacher series)

CPSIA information can be obtained
at www.ICGtesting.com
Printed in the USA
BVHW031721110521
607040BV00007B/948